Unity Game Development Scripting

Write efficient C# scripts to create modular key game elements that are usable for any kind of Unity project

Kyle D'Aoust

PUBLISHING

BIRMINGHAM - MUMBAI

Unity Game Development Scripting

First published: December 2014

Production reference: 1151214

Published by Packt Publishing Ltd.
Livery Place
35 Livery Street
Birmingham B3 2PB, UK.

ISBN 978-1-78355-363-1

www.packtpub.com

Credits

Author
Kyle D'Aoust

Reviewers
Marcieb Balisacan
Paulo Barbeiro
Volodymyr Gerasimov
Dan Lingman
Conor O'Kane
Francesco Sapio

Commissioning Editor
Akram Hussain

Acquisition Editor
Sam Wood

Content Development Editor
Parita Khedekar

Technical Editor
Tanvi Bhatt

Copy Editors
Pranjali Chury
Adithi Shetty

Project Coordinator
Rashi Khivansara

Proofreaders
Simran Bhogal
Maria Gould
Ameesha Green
Paul Hindle

Indexer
Priya Sane

Production Coordinator
Shantanu N. Zagade

Cover Work
Shantanu N. Zagade

About the Author

Kyle D'Aoust has been programming for about 10 years. In 2004, at the age of 14, he taught himself the C++ language. By the end of high school, he had learned Visual Basic and JavaScript as well. In college, he majored in game production and specialized in the Unity engine using C#.

After graduating from college, Kyle started his career with gamifying software. He is currently working as a Serious Games Developer at Quicken Loans, creating games used as training material.

I would like to thank my parents for supporting me in my work.

About the Reviewers

Marcieb Balisacan is an independent game developer, a designer, and a producer working in the Philippines. He has a background in computer science and multimedia, and he has released several games for mobile devices and social networks on the Web since 2006. His passion for game development is equaled only by his passion for music and storytelling, all of which he uses to share his love for the art of creation. He has recently cofounded a game development studio start-up, Full Mana Studios (www.fullmana.com), and is the Lead Game Engineer in Synergy88 Studios, where he is leading the design and development of computer games.

> I would like to acknowledge my newborn son, Aedan Chord, who kept me awake during the review of this book and inspired me to move forward.

Paulo Barbeiro has been involved in digital world development since 1999 as a web designer. During the last 15 years, he has worked with frontend and backend web development, mobile apps, games, and electronic arts, and has taught creative code principles and techniques.

He graduated as a graphic designer, but digital environment development was always a passion, so the natural move was in the direction of computer science, specializing in game development and computer graphics. He believes that there is no border between artistic creation and logical thinking for software development—both elements must work together.

Being a Unity3D user since version 1, Paulo was thrilled to contribute to this book as a technical reviewer. He has also contributed to books about Panda3D by Packt Publishing.

Currently, Paulo resides in São Paulo, Brazil, working as a lead developer for the TicTaskDo mobile app and in SESC SP, organizing events and seminars about digital art, code, and interactive environments.

Volodymyr Gerasimov is a game developer living in Vinnitsya, Ukraine. For the last 5 years, he has studied game design and scripting and applied this to his work as a level designer, producer, and game developer.

Volodymyr graduated from The Art Institute of Vancouver with a diploma in Game Art & Design, and he worked for companies such as Holymountain Games, Best Way, and Gameloft. Currently, he works as an independent game developer on a title for mobile platforms.

He enjoys learning new skills and sharing them with his friends, peers, and the rest of the world by teaching game design and co-authoring books such as *Unity 3.x Scripting*, *Packt Publishing*.

I would like to thank my mentors and peers for keeping up with my overachieving attitude and giving me the energy to stay hungry and foolish in my pursuit of success.

Dan Lingman is currently a Professor of Game Development at Algonquin College in Ottawa, Canada. He became involved in game development in 1981 when he worked on Commodore PET. Building software, especially games, has been his passion for over 30 years. He's worked on all types of software on various platforms for far too many companies to list.

Most recently, he's contributed code to the award-nominated games, *Schrödinger's Cat* and *Raiders of the Lost Quark*. Right now, Dan's focused on creating new methods for procedural dungeon generation and adaptive AIs in Unity 5.0.

Conor O'Kane is a game developer and teacher from Dublin. He is the director of Io Normal, a game development studio based in Melbourne. He lectures at RMIT University in courses covering game design, character modeling and rigging, rapid prototyping, and mobile game development.

Conor lives with his wife and two children in Melbourne. When he is not busy creating video games, he enjoys playing the Irish flute.

Francesco Sapio is an Italian student of Computer Science and Control Engineering with an excellent academic record. He is close to graduating. In the near future, he'll start pursuing a Master of Science degree in Engineering in Artificial Intelligence and Robotics, following his passion for computer science that he has been cultivating since he was 3 years old — when he held his first Mac in his hands, an experience that totally changed his life.

In recent times, he has developed a hotel management system and built websites for hotels with booking engines integrated with the major OTAs portals. Besides this, he is a Unity3D expert and a skilled game designer, as well as an experienced user of the major graphic programs. For several years, he worked as an actor and as a dancer — he was a guest of honor at the Brancaccio theatre in Rome.

He is also a musician and composer, and mostly composes soundtracks for short films and video games. In the recent past, he has helped a lot of young kids to start playing piano. In addition, he is a very active person. He is an animator and gives private lessons in mathematics and music for high school and university students.

Furthermore, he loves maths, philosophy, logic, and puzzle solving, but most of all, creating video games. Owing to his passion for game designing and programming, his dream — with a bit of pride — is to become a famous and successful game designer.

I'm deeply grateful to my parents for their infinite patience and for raising and supporting me. I would like to specially thank my father; without him, I wouldn't be here today. Moreover, I'm thankful to the rest of my family and to my friends, in particular my grandparents, since they always encouraged me to do better in my life with the Latin expressions "Ad Maiora" and "Per aspera ad astra".

Besides this, I would like to thank the team at Packt Publishing, especially my old project coordinator for introducing me to this world and my current project coordinator for her kindness.

Finally, huge thanks to my fiancée; I'm grateful to have your support with me in whatever I do. Love you.

www.PacktPub.com

Support files, eBooks, discount offers, and more

For support files and downloads related to your book, please visit www.PacktPub.com.

Did you know that Packt offers eBook versions of every book published, with PDF and ePub files available? You can upgrade to the eBook version at www.PacktPub.com and as a print book customer, you are entitled to a discount on the eBook copy. Get in touch with us at service@packtpub.com for more details.

At www.PacktPub.com, you can also read a collection of free technical articles, sign up for a range of free newsletters and receive exclusive discounts and offers on Packt books and eBooks.

https://www2.packtpub.com/books/subscription/packtlib

Do you need instant solutions to your IT questions? PacktLib is Packt's online digital book library. Here, you can search, access, and read Packt's entire library of books.

Why subscribe?

- Fully searchable across every book published by Packt
- Copy and paste, print, and bookmark content
- On demand and accessible via a web browser

Free access for Packt account holders

If you have an account with Packt at www.PacktPub.com, you can use this to access PacktLib today and view 9 entirely free books. Simply use your login credentials for immediate access.

Table of Contents

Preface

This book will cover many helpful topics that you can utilize when you create your own games. As a game developer and scripter, you'll end up writing a lot of code that you would not want to write again; this book will help to solve that. You will learn how to make gameplay elements modular so that they can be used again in other projects as well. This book will take what you might already know about gameplay scripting in Unity to the next level.

What this book covers

Chapter 1, *Interactive Input*, gives an in-depth look at how to create controls for both the Xbox 360 Controller and mouse/keyboard inputs. Along with creating those inputs, you'll also create customizable control profiles that the player can use to play your game the way they want to.

Chapter 2, *GUI Time*, will help you create both 2D and 3D GUI elements. This covers health bars, player data, hovering 3D health bars, 3D damage reports, enemy names, and so on.

Chapter 3, *Expandable Item Classes*, will teach you how to create in-game item classes for self, melee, and projectile items. Then, you'll create a classification system for these items to determine what they do.

Chapter 4, *Inventory*, will teach you a way to create an inventory system for your game. In this system, there'll be common inventory elements created such as adding items, removing items, and creating quick-select items. Finally, you'll also create a way to show the inventory on the GUI.

Chapter 5, *Enemy and Friendly AIs*, will demonstrate how to create a dynamic AI. It will cover what a finite state machine is and also what a behavior tree is. This AI system will handle behaviors, actions, animations, pathfinding, and also a waypoint system.

Chapter 6, Keeping Score, covers how to create, track, and save stats for the player. You'll also create a system for achievements for those stats as well.

Chapter 7, Creating Save and Load Systems, covers how to create systems to save and load from a flat file as well as an XML file. Then, you'll take these systems and implement them on a checkpoint-based save system and an anywhere/anytime saving system.

Chapter 8, Aural Integration, covers the creation of systems that will handle background music, atmospheric sounds, and sound effects. These systems are a playlist system, a randomized system, and an event-driven system.

Chapter 9, Game Settings, covers how to create customizable configurations for audio and video settings. You'll create the ability to save and load these settings by using PlayerPrefs.

Chapter 10, Putting It All Together, will put almost everything you've learned from the previous chapters into a small game. By taking elements from the previous chapters, you'll create a short First Person Action RPG.

What you need for this book

For this book, all that you'll need is Unity3D to write all of the scripts needed and Notepad++ to create XML files. While you may be able to create XML files in other programs, I use Notepad++ because it's easy to use and is a nice program to have as a programmer.

Who this book is for

This book can be used by someone who already has some programming or scripting knowledge and wants to get into game development using Unity3D. If you've already been using Unity3D for some time, this book may be of use to you as well as it has a theme to create modular gameplay elements.

Conventions

In this book, you will find a number of text styles that distinguish between different kinds of information. Here are some examples of these styles and an explanation of their meaning.

Code words in text, database table names, folder names, filenames, file extensions, pathnames, dummy URLs, user input, and Twitter handles are shown as follows: "The reset function will use our `SetDefaultValues()` function as well as reset a couple of our other variables."

A block of code is set as follows:

```
void Reset()
{
  SetDefaultValues();
  ShowPopup = false;
  PreviousKey = KeyCode.None;
}
```

New terms and **important words** are shown in bold. Words that you see on the screen, for example, in menus or dialog boxes, appear in the text like this: "Open up the **Axes** dropdown by clicking on the arrow next to it."

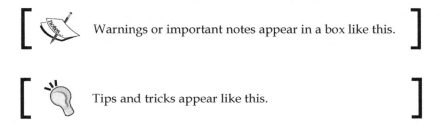

Warnings or important notes appear in a box like this.

Tips and tricks appear like this.

Reader feedback

Feedback from our readers is always welcome. Let us know what you think about this book—what you liked or disliked. Reader feedback is important for us as it helps us develop titles that you will really get the most out of.

To send us general feedback, simply e-mail `feedback@packtpub.com`, and mention the book's title in the subject of your message.

If there is a topic that you have expertise in and you are interested in either writing or contributing to a book, see our author guide at `www.packtpub.com/authors`.

Customer support

Now that you are the proud owner of a Packt book, we have a number of things to help you to get the most from your purchase.

Downloading the example code

You can download the example code files from your account at http://www.packtpub.com for all the Packt Publishing books you have purchased. If you purchased this book elsewhere, you can visit http://www.packtpub.com/support and register to have the files e-mailed directly to you.

Errata

Although we have taken every care to ensure the accuracy of our content, mistakes do happen. If you find a mistake in one of our books—maybe a mistake in the text or the code—we would be grateful if you could report this to us. By doing so, you can save other readers from frustration and help us improve subsequent versions of this book. If you find any errata, please report them by visiting http://www.packtpub.com/submit-errata, selecting your book, clicking on the **Errata Submission Form** link, and entering the details of your errata. Once your errata are verified, your submission will be accepted and the errata will be uploaded to our website or added to any list of existing errata under the Errata section of that title.

To view the previously submitted errata, go to https://www.packtpub.com/books/content/support and enter the name of the book in the search field. The required information will appear under the **Errata** section.

Piracy

Piracy of copyrighted material on the Internet is an ongoing problem across all media. At Packt, we take the protection of our copyright and licenses very seriously. If you come across any illegal copies of our works in any form on the Internet, please provide us with the location address or website name immediately so that we can pursue a remedy.

Please contact us at copyright@packtpub.com with a link to the suspected pirated material.

We appreciate your help in protecting our authors and our ability to bring you valuable content.

Questions

If you have a problem with any aspect of this book, you can contact us at questions@packtpub.com, and we will do our best to address the problem.

1
Interactive Input

Before we start creating our game, it is a good idea to figure out our controls. We'll create a script that will hold our inputs, and create control profiles for both the keyboard/mouse as well as the **Xbox 360 Controller**. Then, we'll add functionalities to be able to switch between the profiles and customize them as well. Control configurations like these are a key element to games, especially PC games.

In this chapter, we will cover the following topics:

- Creating controls for the Xbox 360 Controller
- Creating controls for a keyboard
- Writing a function to detect whether our controller device is plugged in
- Customizing our controls
- Letting players switch controls
- Switching controls with **Graphical User Interface (GUI)** buttons
- Resetting controls back to *factory settings*

Picking the controls

Before we start creating our game, we should decide how the player will play the game. The controls are one of the most key parts of a game.

Mapping the needed controls

For the game that we will create, we will need several controls. Some are already included in the input manager within Unity, while some are not. The following table shows what default controls we will be using, and what buttons we'll use for them:

Action	Keyboard/mouse	Xbox 360 Controller
Movement	*WASD* keys	Left thumbstick
Rotate camera	Mouse	Right thumbstick
Item bar buttons	*1234* keys	Directional pad
Inventory	The *I* key	The *A* button
Pause game	The *Esc* key	The *Start* button
Attack / use an item	The left mouse button	The right trigger
Aim	The right mouse button	The left trigger

Checking the input manager

In the following screenshot, you can see that there are default inputs already implemented, which we can use for the movement, rotate camera, attack/use item, and aim actions:

As you can see, we still need to add inputs for the inventory, pause game, and item bar buttons. We will also need to make sure that the inputs we enter will support inputs from the Xbox 360 Controller.

Checking the Xbox 360 Controller inputs

Before we add stuff into the input manager, we should take a look at what the inputs are on the Xbox 360 Controller. This will help us integrate the controller inputs in the input manager, as well as give us an insight on how to code the controller inputs.

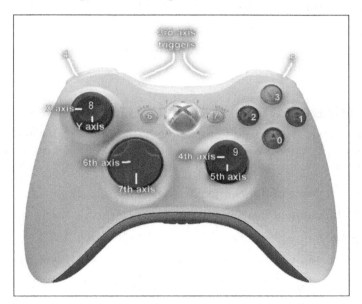

Adding additional controller inputs

To get started, access your input manager by navigating to the **Edit** menu, hovering over **Project Settings**, and clicking on **Input**. Open up the **Axes** dropdown by clicking on the arrow next to it and change the number in the **Size** parameter to be a value higher. This will add another input at the bottom of the list, which we can use for one of our types of inputs.

By default, by creating a new type of input, the input manager duplicates the bottom input. So open it and we'll make our changes. Follow these steps to create our new input:

1. Change the value of the **Name** parameter to A_360.
2. Change the value of the **Positive Button** parameter to joystick button 0.

Adding a start button and trigger inputs

As you can see, it's fairly easy to add an Xbox 360 input in the input manager. You can follow the same steps to add the start button; just change the value of the **Name** parameter to Start_360 and the value of the positive button to joystick button 7. For the two triggers, you will need to follow slightly different steps:

1. Change the value of the **Name** parameter to Triggers_360.
2. Change the value of the **Sensitivity** parameter to 0.001.
3. Check the **Invert** parameter.
4. Change the value of the **Type** parameter to **Joystick Axis**.
5. Change the value of the **Axis** parameter to **3rd Axis (Joysticks and Scrollwheel)**.

Adding directional pad inputs

For the directional pad, we'll need to make the horizontal buttons and vertical buttons separately, but these will both be similar to how we set up the triggers. First, we will create the horizontal directional pad input:

1. Change the value of the **Name** parameter to HorizDpad_360.
2. Change the value of the **Sensitivity** parameter to 1.
3. Change the value of the **Type** parameter to **Joystick Axis**.
4. Change the value of the **Axis** parameter to **6th Axis (Joysticks)**.

For the vertical directional pad input, you can follow the exact same steps as we did for the horizontal directional pad input; just change the value of **Name** to VertDpad_360 and change the value of **Axis** to 7th Axis (Joysticks). This completes the Xbox 360 Controller inputs; all that's left are the PC inputs.

Adding PC control inputs

Most of our PC control inputs are already integrated into the input manager; all that is left are the number keys, *I* key, and *Esc* key.

You can actually follow the same steps as at the beginning of this chapter, when we added the Xbox 360 buttons. For the number keys you'll want to change each of their names to num1, num2, num3, and num4. As for their positive button parameters, change their names to 1, 2, 3, and 4, accordingly.

The *I* key name will be I_Key and its positive button parameter will be i. For the *Esc* key, we will want the **Name** parameter to be Esc_Key and its positive button parameter will be escape.

Housing our control script

Now that we have our control inputs set up, we'll set up our script that will house all our control-based scripting.

Creating and naming the script

Create a new script either by right-clicking on **Project Window**, hovering over the **Create** tab, and clicking on the C# script, or by navigating through the **Assets** menu and creating the new C# script this way. Once you have done this, rename the script ControlConfig.

Formatting the script

After you have created and named the script, open it. Ensure that the class name, ControlConfig, is the same as the filename. You'll see that Unity has created the start and update functions for use already. You should delete both of these functions, which will leave you with an open and empty class.

Creating the device detector

The first function we'll create is one that will detect whether we actually have a gamepad plugged in. Unity inherently gives us a way to make this very easy.

Adding the variables needed

First, we'll add variables that we'll use in the detection and identification functions. Add these to the top of your script, just after the class declaration:

```
bool isControllerConnected = false;
public string Controller = "";
```

This Boolean will be used in later functions to determine whether there is a gamepad connected. The string will be used to hold the name of the gamepad connected.

Creating the detection function

Our next step is to add the `DetectController` function. This will use the Boolean we created earlier and check whether there is a gamepad connected. Add the following code to your script:

```
void DetectController()
{
  try
  {
    if(Input.GetJoystickNames()[0] != null)
    {
      isControllerConnected = true;
      IdentifyController();
    }
  }
  catch
  {
    isControllerConnected = false;
  }
}
```

This function uses the `GetJoystickNames` function of the input, which gets and returns an array of strings, which consists of the names of the connected gamepads. We use this to set our Boolean to true or false; true meaning there's a device connected and false meaning that the game couldn't detect a device. The reason we use a try-catch expression is because if there is no gamepad connected `Input.GetJoystickNames()` will give you an `IndexOutOfRangeException` error.

Creating the identifier function

Our last step in creating the device detector will be to add the ability to identify the gamepad connected. Add this function to the script, just below the `DetectController` function:

```
void IdentifyController()
{
  Controller = Input.GetJoystickNames()[0];
}
```

As you can see, we are assigning the name of the gamepad connected to our `Controller` variable. To use this function, call it within the `DetectController` function, in the `if` statement, where we set `isControllerConnected` to `true`.

Let's get set and show them

The next step in our `Control` script is to set up our controls to be able to customize what they do, and display what each control does.

Adding variables for each control

At the top of your script, after your other variables, add these new variables:

```
public string PC_Move, PC_Rotate, PC_Item1, PC_Item2, PC_Item3, PC_
Item4, PC_Inv, PC_Pause, PC_AttackUse, PC_Aim;
public string Xbox_Move, Xbox_Rotate, Xbox_Item1, Xbox_Item2, Xbox_
Item3, Xbox_Item4, Xbox_Inv, Xbox_Pause, Xbox_AttackUse, Xbox_Aim;
```

We will use these variables to display our controls on the screen. Later, we'll use them for customization as well. Add this code to assign the default values to our new variables:

```
void SetDefaultValues()
{
  if(!isControllerConnected)
  {
    PC_Move = "WASD";
    PC_Rotate = "Mouse";
    PC_Item1 = "1";
    PC_Item2 = "2";
    PC_Item3 = "3";
    PC_Item4 = "4";
    PC_Inv = "I";
    PC_Pause = "Escape";
    PC_AttackUse = "Left Mouse Button";
    PC_Aim = "Right Mouse Button";
  }
  else
  {
    PC_Move = "WASD";
    PC_Rotate = "Mouse";
    PC_Item1 = "1";
    PC_Item2 = "2";
    PC_Item3 = "3";
    PC_Item4 = "4";
    PC_Inv = "I";
    PC_Pause = "Escape";
    PC_AttackUse = "Left Mouse Button";
    PC_Aim = "Right Mouse Button";
```

```
        Xbox_Move = "Left Thumbstick";
        Xbox_Rotate = "Right Thumbstick";
        Xbox_Item1 = "D-Pad Up";
        Xbox_Item2 = "D-Pad Down";
        Xbox_Item3 = "D-Pad Left";
        Xbox_Item4 = "D-Pad Right";
        Xbox_Inv = "A Button";
        Xbox_Pause = "Start Button";
        Xbox_AttackUse = "Right Trigger";
        Xbox_Aim = "Left Trigger";
    }
}
```

We will set these variables in a function because later we will use this function again to reset the controls if they are customized. The function uses our isControllerConnected variable to determine whether a gamepad is plugged in or not, and then assigns the appropriate data.

Adding a function to display the variables

Next, we will use the OnGUI function to display our controls onto the screen. We will create a menu that will show each action and their controls for a PC and Xbox 360 Controller, very similar to the table shown at the beginning of this chapter. Add this code to the bottom of your script:

```
void OnGUI()
{
  GUI.BeginGroup(new Rect(Screen.width/2 - 300, Screen.height / 2 -
300, 600, 400));
  GUI.Box(new Rect(0,0,600,400), "Controls");
  GUI.Label(new Rect(205, 40, 20, 20), "PC");
  GUI.Label(new Rect(340, 40, 125, 20), "Xbox 360 Controller");

  GUI.Label(new Rect(25, 75, 125, 20), "Movement: ");
  GUI.Button(new Rect(150, 75, 135, 20), PC_Move);
  GUI.Button(new Rect(325, 75, 135, 20), Xbox_Move);

  GUI.Label(new Rect(25, 100, 125, 20), "Rotation: ");
  GUI.Button(new Rect(150, 100, 135, 20), PC_Rotate);
  GUI.Button(new Rect(325, 100, 135, 20), Xbox_Rotate);

  GUI.Label(new Rect(25, 125, 125, 20), "Item 1: ");
  GUI.Button(new Rect(150, 125, 135, 20), PC_Item1);
  GUI.Button(new Rect(325, 125, 135, 20), Xbox_Item1);
```

```
GUI.Label(new Rect(25, 150, 125, 20), "Item 2: ");
GUI.Button(new Rect(150, 150, 135, 20), PC_Item2);
GUI.Button(new Rect(325, 150, 135, 20), Xbox_Item2);

GUI.Label(new Rect(25, 175, 125, 20), "Item 3: ");
GUI.Button(new Rect(150, 175, 135, 20), PC_Item3);
GUI.Button(new Rect(325, 175, 135, 20), Xbox_Item3);

GUI.Label(new Rect(25, 200, 125, 20), "Item 4: ");
GUI.Button(new Rect(150, 200, 135, 20), PC_Item4);
GUI.Button(new Rect(325, 200, 135, 20), Xbox_Item4);

GUI.Label(new Rect(25, 225, 125, 20), "Inventory: ");
GUI.Button(new Rect(150, 225, 135, 20), PC_Inv);
GUI.Button(new Rect(325, 225, 135, 20), Xbox_Inv);

GUI.Label(new Rect(25, 250, 125, 20), "Pause Game: ");
GUI.Button(new Rect(150, 250, 135, 20), PC_Pause);
GUI.Button(new Rect(325, 250, 135, 20), Xbox_Pause);

GUI.Label(new Rect(25, 275, 125, 20), "Attack/Use: ");
GUI.Button(new Rect(150, 275, 135, 20), PC_AttackUse);
GUI.Button(new Rect(325, 275, 135, 20), Xbox_AttackUse);

GUI.Label(new Rect(25, 300, 125, 20), "Aim: ");
GUI.Button(new Rect(150, 300, 135, 20), PC_Aim);
GUI.Button(new Rect(325, 300, 135, 20), Xbox_Aim);
GUI.EndGroup();
}
```

The preceding code is fairly self-explanatory; we use GUI labels to show what actions the player can do, then use the GUI buttons to show what inputs the actions are mapped to. Later, we'll use these buttons as a way to customize our controls.

Let's switch!

Now, we'll create a way for the player to switch between PC and Xbox 360 Controller controls.

Creating control profiles

To create our profiles, we'll need to add a new variable. Add the following **enum** to the top of our script, before the class declaration:

```
public enum ControlProfile { PC, Controller };
```

Add it to your variables as well, like this:

```
public ControlProfile cProfile;
```

Finally, go to the DetectController() function. Add this line of code before the line of code where you call the IdentifyController() function in the if statement:

```
cProfile = ControlProfile.Controller;
```

After this, add an else statement to the if statement with another line of code after it:

```
else
  cProfile = ControlProfile.PC;
```

We are setting our enum variable in the DetectController() function to give us a default control profile. This is a fast and effective way to give our player the best control profile possible.

Adding a profile switching function

Next, we'll add a function that we can call to manually switch the control profile. Add this function to our code:

```
void SwitchProfile (ControlProfile Switcher)
{
  cProfile = Switcher;
}
```

We can call this function later to let the player choose between using the keyboard/mouse or the Xbox 360 Controller.

Adding the GUI interaction function

Now, we'll add a button to the bottom right of our controls page to let the player pick between the keyboard/mouse and Xbox 360 Controller. Add this code to your onGUI() function, just before the line where we end the group:

```
GUI.Label(new Rect(450, 345, 125, 20), "Current Controls");
if(GUI.Button(new Rect(425, 370, 135, 20), cProfile.ToString()))
```

```
{
  if(cProfile == ControlProfile.Controller)
    SwitchProfile(ControlProfile.PC);
  else
    SwitchProfile(ControlProfile.Controller);
}
```

The text on the button will display which current control profile is being used. When the player clicks on the button, it will switch the control profile.

Customization is key

It's time to customize our controls! We'll go over a couple of ways to add customization to our controls. Unity doesn't allow us to edit the input properties while in-game, so we will create a couple of ways to change the controls ourselves. In our game, we will utilize both these ways.

Swapping control schemes

Our first method will be to switch between preset control schemes. To start off, we'll add a bunch of variables that we will use for our controls:

```
string ControlScheme;
public KeyCode pcItem1, pcItem2, pcItem3, pcItem4, pcInv, pcPause,
pcAttackUse, pcAim, xInv, xPause;
```

Since we can't modify the input properties, some of our controls will not be customized, such as movement, camera rotation, Xbox 360 Controller attack/use, and Xbox 360 Controller item switching. Next, we will need to set some default values to these variables; we'll modify our SetDefaultValues() function to look like this:

```
void SetDefaultValues()
{
  ControlScheme = "Scheme A";
  if(!isControllerConnected)
  {
    PC_Move = "WASD";
    PC_Rotate = "Mouse";
    PC_Item1 = "1";
    PC_Item2 = "2";
    PC_Item3 = "3";
    PC_Item4 = "4";
    PC_Inv = "I";
```

```
        PC_Pause = "Escape";
        PC_AttackUse = "Left Mouse Button";
        PC_Aim = "Right Mouse Button";


        pcItem1 = KeyCode.Alpha1;
        pcItem2 = KeyCode.Alpha2;
        pcItem3 = KeyCode.Alpha3;
        pcItem4 = KeyCode.Alpha4;
        pcInv = KeyCode.I;
        pcPause = KeyCode.Escape;
        pcAttackUse = KeyCode.Mouse0;
        pcAim = KeyCode.Mouse1;
    }
    else
    {
        PC_Move = "WASD";
        PC_Rotate = "Mouse";
        PC_Item1 = "1";
        PC_Item2 = "2";
        PC_Item3 = "3";
        PC_Item4 = "4";
        PC_Inv = "I";
        PC_Pause = "Escape";
        PC_AttackUse = "Left Mouse Button";
        PC_Aim = "Right Mouse Button";
        Xbox_Move = "Left Thumbstick";
        Xbox_Rotate = "Right Thumbstick";
        Xbox_Item1 = "D-Pad Up";
        Xbox_Item2 = "D-Pad Down";
        Xbox_Item3 = "D-Pad Left";
        Xbox_Item4 = "D-Pad Right";
        Xbox_Inv = "A Button";
        Xbox_Pause = "Start Button";
        Xbox_AttackUse = "Right Trigger";
        Xbox_Aim = "Left Trigger";

        pcItem1 = KeyCode.Alpha1;
        pcItem2 = KeyCode.Alpha2;
        pcItem3 = KeyCode.Alpha3;
        pcItem4 = KeyCode.Alpha4;
        pcInv = KeyCode.I;
        pcPause = KeyCode.Escape;
        pcAttackUse = KeyCode.Mouse0;
        pcAim = KeyCode.Mouse1;
```

```
    xInv = KeyCode.I;
    xPause = KeyCode.Escape;
    }
  }
```

Next, we will add a function to our script that will allow the player to switch between control schemes:

```
void SwitchControlScheme(string Scheme)
{
  switch(Scheme)
  {
  case "Scheme A":
    SetDefaultValues();
  break;
  case "Scheme B":
    if(!isControllerConnected)
    {
      PC_Move = "WASD";
      PC_Rotate = "Mouse";
      PC_Item1 = "Numpad 1";
      PC_Item2 = "Numpad 2";
      PC_Item3 = "Numpad 3";
      PC_Item4 = "Numpad 4";
      PC_Inv = "Numpad +";
      PC_Pause = "Enter";
      PC_AttackUse = "Right Mouse Button";
      PC_Aim = "Left Mouse Button";

      pcItem1 = KeyCode.Keypad1;
      pcItem2 = KeyCode.Keypad2;
      pcItem3 = KeyCode.Keypad3;
      pcItem4 = KeyCode.Keypad4;
      pcInv = KeyCode.KeypadPlus;
      pcPause = KeyCode.Return;
      pcAttackUse = KeyCode.Mouse1;
      pcAim = KeyCode.Mouse0;
    }
    else
    {
      PC_Move = "WASD";
      PC_Rotate = "Mouse";
      PC_Item1 = "Numpad 1";
      PC_Item2 = "Numpad 2";
      PC_Item3 = "Numpad 3";
```

```
                PC_Item4 = "Numpad 4";
                PC_Inv = "Numpad +";
                PC_Pause = "Enter";
                PC_AttackUse = "Right Mouse Button";
                PC_Aim = "Left Mouse Button";
                Xbox_Move = "Left Thumbstick";
                Xbox_Rotate = "Right Thumbstick";
                Xbox_Item1 = "D-Pad Up";
                Xbox_Item2 = "D-Pad Down";
                Xbox_Item3 = "D-Pad Left";
                Xbox_Item4 = "D-Pad Right";
                Xbox_Inv = "B Button";
                Xbox_Pause = "Back Button";
                Xbox_AttackUse = "Right Trigger";
                Xbox_Aim = "Left Trigger";

                pcItem1 = KeyCode.Keypad1;
                pcItem2 = KeyCode.Keypad2;
                pcItem3 = KeyCode.Keypad3;
                pcItem4 = KeyCode.Keypad4;
                pcInv = KeyCode.KeypadPlus;
                pcPause = KeyCode.Return;
                pcAttackUse = KeyCode.Mouse1;
                pcAim = KeyCode.Mouse0;
                xInv = KeyCode.JoystickButton1;
                xPause = KeyCode.JoystickButton6;
            }
        break;
        }
    }
```

As you can see, this function is very similar to our SetDefaultValues() function; it acts the same way. SwitchControlScheme() takes a string that determines which control scheme to use and then assigns the appropriate data. The first scheme is the default control scheme, while the other one is a new scheme. The new scheme changes the following:

- Item keys are now on the keypad
- Inventory buttons are now the + key and *B* key
- Attack/use inputs are switched on the mouse
- Pause has been changed to the *Enter* key and the Backspace key

Adding a control switch button to the GUI

Lastly, we'll need to add a GUI button to our OnGUI function to allow the player to switch control schemes. Add the following before the line that ends the group:

```
GUI.Label(new Rect(15, 345, 125, 20), "Current Control Scheme");
if(GUI.Button(new Rect(25, 370, 135, 20), ControlScheme))
{
  if(ControlScheme == "Scheme A")
  {
    SwitchControlScheme("B");
    ControlScheme = "Scheme B";
  }
  else
  {
    SwitchControlScheme("A");
    ControlScheme = "Scheme A";
  }
}
```

This button, when clicked, will call the SwitchControlScheme() function and pass it a letter determining the control scheme being used.

Cycling control inputs

Our next method of customization will let the player click on one of the GUI buttons in our controls, and pick another control to switch it. To start off, we'll add variables that we'll use to hold the original values of our controls. The last two variables will be used to allow us to customize our controls:

```
private KeyCode orig_pcItem1, orig_pcItem2, orig_pcItem3, orig_
pcItem4, orig_pcInv, orig_pcPause, orig_xInv, orig_xPause;
bool ShowPopup = false;
KeyCode PreviousKey;
```

In the SetDefaultValues function, assign these variables to our previous control variables in both the if and else statements:

```
orig_pcItem1 = pcItem1;
orig_pcItem2 = pcItem2;
orig_pcItem3 = pcItem3;
orig_pcItem4 = pcItem4;
orig_pcInv = pcInv;
orig_pcPause = pcPause;
```

Assign the Xbox 360 Controller controls in the `else` statement:

```
orig_xInv = xInv;
orig_xPause = xPause;
```

Next, we are going to add a function that we'll call to switch our keys:

```
void SetNewKey(KeyCode KeyToSet, KeyCode SetTo)
{
  switch(KeyToSet)
  {
  case KeyCode.Alpha1:
    pcItem1 = SetTo;
    PC_Item1 = SetString(pcItem1.ToString());
    break;
  case KeyCode.Alpha2:
    pcItem2 = SetTo;
    PC_Item2 = SetString(pcItem2.ToString());
    break;
  case KeyCode.Alpha3:
    pcItem3 = SetTo;
    PC_Item3 = SetString(pcItem3.ToString());
    break;
  case KeyCode.Alpha4:
    pcItem4 = SetTo;
    PC_Item4 = SetString(pcItem4.ToString());
    break;
  case KeyCode.I:
    pcInv = SetTo;
    PC_Inv = SetString(pcInv.ToString());
    break;
  case KeyCode.Escape:
    pcPause = SetTo;
    PC_Pause = SetString(pcPause.ToString());
    break;
  case KeyCode.JoystickButton1:
    xInv = SetTo;
    Xbox_Inv = SetString(xInv.ToString());
    break;
  case KeyCode.JoystickButton6:
    xPause = SetTo;
    Xbox_Pause = SetString(xPause.ToString());
    break;
  }
}
```

This new function takes in two properties: the first one will be what `KeyCode` we set and the second one will be what `KeyCode` we are setting the key to. You can see that we also set our string variables, which are used in the GUI with another function. We'll create that function now:

```
string SetString(string SetTo)
{
  switch(SetTo)
  {
  case "Alpha1":
    SetTo = "1";
    break;
  case "Alpha2":
    SetTo = "2";
    break;
  case "Alpha3":
    SetTo = "3";
    break;
  case "Alpha4":
    SetTo = "4";
    break;
  case "Return":
    SetTo = "Enter";
    break;
  case "Escape":
    SetTo = "Escape";
    break;
  case "I":
    SetTo = "I";
    break;
  case "JoystickButton6":
    SetTo = "Start Button";
    break;
  case "JoystickButton1":
    SetTo = "A Button";
    break;
  }
  return SetTo;
}
```

Now in our OnGUI function, we'll need to adjust some of our code. Before we start our controls group, we will check whether our controls pop up is activated. Add the if statement to our code and encapsulate the Controls Group:

```
if(!ShowPopup)
{
```

Next, we'll edit some of our GUI buttons to allow customization. Start with the PC_Item1 button and change it to this code:

```
if(GUI.Button(new Rect(150, 125, 135, 20), PC_Item1))
{
  ShowPopup = true;
  PreviousKey = pcItem1;
}
```

Do the same thing for the following buttons:

- PC_Item2
- PC_Item3
- PC_Item4
- PC_Pause
- PC_Inv
- Xbox_Inv
- Xbox_Pause

Set **ShowPopup** to true and PreviousKey to its expected value, accordingly, such as pcItem2, pcItem3, pcItem4, and so on. Place a closing bracket afterwards to close the if statement that we created earlier.

Adding the controls pop up to the GUI

It's time to add our controls pop up to the GUI. This is where the player will select what control to swap. To do this, we will add an else statement, extending our if statement, to create the pop up:

```
else
{
  GUI.BeginGroup(new Rect(Screen.width/2 - 300, Screen.height / 2 -
300, 600, 400));
  GUI.Box(new Rect(0,0,600,400), "Pick A Control to Switch");
  if(GUI.Button(new Rect(150, 125, 135, 20), "1"))
  {
```

```
      SetNewKey(PreviousKey, orig_pcItem1);
      ShowPopup = false;
    }
    if(GUI.Button(new Rect(150, 150, 135, 20), "2"))
    {
      SetNewKey(PreviousKey, orig_pcItem2);
      ShowPopup = false;
    }
    if(GUI.Button(new Rect(150, 175, 135, 20), "3"))
    {
      SetNewKey(PreviousKey, orig_pcItem3);
      ShowPopup = false;
    }
    if(GUI.Button(new Rect(150, 200, 135, 20), "4"))
    {
      SetNewKey(PreviousKey, orig_pcItem4);
      ShowPopup = false;
    }
    if(GUI.Button(new Rect(150, 225, 135, 20), "I"))
    {
      SetNewKey(PreviousKey, orig_pcInv);
      ShowPopup = false;
    }
    if(GUI.Button(new Rect(150, 250, 135, 20), "Escape"))
    {
      SetNewKey(PreviousKey, orig_pcPause);
      ShowPopup = false;
    }
    if(GUI.Button(new Rect(325, 225, 135, 20), "A Button"))
    {
      SetNewKey(PreviousKey, orig_xInv);
      ShowPopup = false;
    }
    if(GUI.Button(new Rect(325, 250, 135, 20), "Start Button"))
    {
      SetNewKey(PreviousKey, orig_xPause);
      ShowPopup = false;
    }
    GUI.EndGroup();
}
```

When the player clicks on one of these new buttons, the SetNewKey function is called. When called, we pass PreviousKey, which is the key the player is customizing, as well as the key they select, which is the new value of PreviousKey. This is a great and simple way to change controls, which makes it simple for the player.

Resetting the controls

In this section, we will add the ability to allow the player to reset the controls to their default values.

Adding the Reset function

The reset function will use our SetDefaultValues() function as well as reset a couple of our other variables:

```
void Reset()
{
  SetDefaultValues();
  ShowPopup = false;
  PreviousKey = KeyCode.None;
}
```

Here, we call our SetDefaultValues() function, and then reset some other variables. Resetting the ShowPopup Boolean and our PreviousKey KeyCode will ensure that everything related to customization of controls has been reset.

Adding the Reset input

Now, we'll make a GUI button that will call the Reset function. Add this just before the line of code that ends the GUI group in the OnGUI() function's if statement:

```
if(GUI.Button(new Rect(230, 370, 135, 20), "Reset Controls"))
{
  Reset();
}
```

When the player clicks on this button, the controls will be set to their default values. Here is the finished product of the script that you just created:

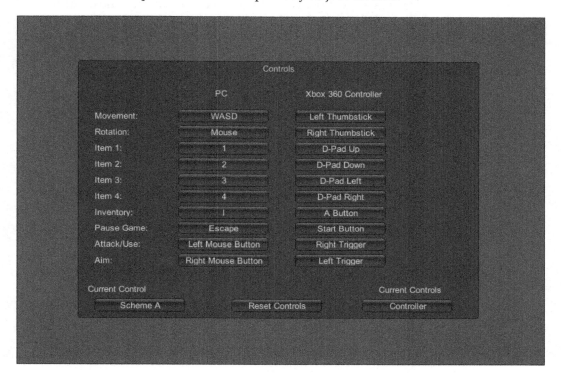

	Controls	
	PC	Xbox 360 Controller
Movement:	WASD	Left Thumbstick
Rotation:	Mouse	Right Thumbstick
Item 1:	1	D-Pad Up
Item 2:	2	D-Pad Down
Item 3:	3	D-Pad Left
Item 4:	4	D-Pad Right
Inventory:	I	A Button
Pause Game:	Escape	Start Button
Attack/Use:	Left Mouse Button	Right Trigger
Aim:	Right Mouse Button	Left Trigger

Current Control Current Controls
Scheme A Reset Controls Controller

Playtesting

Now for the most important part, playtesting! Go ahead and play with the GUI buttons and make sure everything works as it is supposed to. Add the Debug.Log statements to where you think you may have problems and see which variable is set to what. Plug in your Xbox 360 Controller and make sure that it detects your controller.

Downloading the example code

You can download the example code files from your account at http://www.packtpub.com for all the Packt Publishing books you have purchased. If you purchased this book elsewhere, you can visit http://www.packtpub.com/support and register to have the files e-mailed directly to you.

Summary

In this chapter, you learned a great deal about how to create and handle control schemes. You also learned how to change preset control schemes, as well as swap the controls. You can now create a game that will support both the keyboard/mouse and Xbox 360 Controller. This is something that is pivotal to games and game design; not everyone likes to use non-customizable controls.

In the next chapter, we'll go over how to utilize the GUI more in depth. You will learn about how to create 3D GUI elements as well as 2D elements. Later on in this book, we will use these new GUI elements to create a more engaging experience.

2
GUI Time

In video games, the GUI is one of the most important parts of the game. It's where you see how much health you have, what level you are at, how much gold you're carrying, and so on. It's how you gather information on your character and the world you are in.

In this chapter, we'll be covering the following topics:

- Both 2D and 3D GUI elements
- How to create GUI buttons
- How to create a 2D health bar
- Tracking the player's level by using a GUI label
- Using two GUI boxes to make an experience bar
- Creating a 3D health bar
- Showing 3D damage reports
- Showing enemy name tags

A traditional 2D UI

To start our GUI programming, we'll create some buttons, a health bar, a level counter, and an experience counter. All of these are common in a variety of video games and are key elements to game design.

Setting up our scene

Since in this part of the chapter we will be dealing with 3D space, we'll need to set up a scene to test with. We'll only need a basic test level, so create a new scene and name it `Chapter 2`. Add a cube or plane for the floor, a directional light, a GameObject for our enemy, and two quads. This is what my scene looks like:

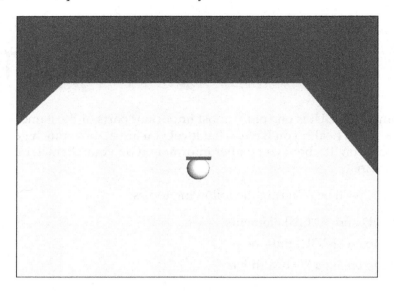

Set the two quads in the same position just above your enemy object and rotate one of them by 180 degrees so that the two quads look like one object. Drag one of the quads onto the other, making a parent-child object. Now that our scene is ready, let's get to the scripting.

Housing our 2D UI

Before we start creating our 2D UI, let's make the script to house it all. Create a new C# script and name it `GUI_2D`. Inside the script, remove the `Update` function. Add a `OnGUI()` function. Finally, add `System.Collections.Generic` to your using statements; we'll need this for some of our variables.

Creating GUI buttons

Our first step in creating 2D buttons in our GUI will be to add these variables:

```
List<Rect> SkillButtons = new List<Rect>();
List<Rect> ItemButtons = new List<Rect>();
```

We will use these two `List` arrays as containers to hold the rectangles for our buttons. For now, they aren't public but if you wanted to expose them to **Inspector**, you could make them public.

Next, we'll need to add rectangles to our lists. Add this block of code to our `Start()` function:

```
SkillButtons.Add(new Rect(Screen.width/2 + 50, Screen.height/2 + 333,
55, 55));
SkillButtons.Add(new Rect(Screen.width/2 + 105, Screen.height/2 +
333, 55, 55));
SkillButtons.Add(new Rect(Screen.width/2 + 160, Screen.height/2 +
333, 55, 55));
ItemButtons.Add(new Rect(Screen.width/2 - 160, Screen.height/2 + 333,
55, 55));
ItemButtons.Add(new Rect(Screen.width/2 - 105, Screen.height/2 + 333,
55, 55));
ItemButtons.Add(new Rect(Screen.width/2 - 50, Screen.height/2 + 333,
55, 55));
```

Here, we will add three buttons to each of our lists. We place our skill buttons to the right of the center of the screen, and we place the item buttons to the left of the center of the screen. Also, all of our buttons have a width and height of 55.

Our last step in creating our buttons is to draw them. We will add this code to our `OnGUI()` function:

```
GUI.Button(SkillButtons[0], "Skill A");
GUI.Button(SkillButtons[1], "Skill B");
GUI.Button(SkillButtons[2], "Skill C");
GUI.Button(ItemButtons[0], "Item A");
GUI.Button(ItemButtons[1], "Item B");
GUI.Button(ItemButtons[2], "Item C");
```

What each of these lines does is draw our button at the location of our rectangles, which we stored in our lists. They also provide text to be displayed on the button; we will use placeholder text as an example.

Creating a health bar

To create a health bar, we will use a GUI box. First, we'll need to add a few variables to calculate our health and the length of the bar:

```
public float currentHP = 100;
public float maxHP = 100;
public float currentBarLength;
public float maxBarLength = 100;
```

We have two variables for our health and bar length: one for the current amount and the other for the maximum amount. Our variables are set to `public` so that we can access them from outside our script.

Finally, to make the health bar, we'll need to add a couple of lines to the `OnGUI()` function to draw it on the screen:

```
currentBarLength = currentHP * maxBarLength / maxHP;
GUI.Box(new Rect(Screen.width/2 - 20, Screen.height/2 + 300,
currentBarLength, 25f), "");
```

The first line of the code will draw our health bar. We set its location to be just above our buttons we created earlier. The second line of the code calculates how long the health bar will be. It multiplies the current amount of health by the maximum bar length, and then divides it by the maximum amount of health. All of these are variables that we've set to `100`, but can be modified to make the bar bigger or smaller.

Level counter

Our level counter will be used to show the player's current level. It's a simple yet gratifying GUI element for the player. We'll only need one variable for the counter:

```
public int currentLevel = 1;
public GUIStyle myStyle;
```

We'll use `currentLevel` to show the player's current level. The `GUIStyle` variable will be used to access the properties of our GUI label. To draw this on the screen, we'll use a GUI label; add this line of code to the `OnGUI()` function:

```
GUI.Label(new Rect(Screen.width/2 + 15, Screen.height/2 + 335, 30,
30), currentLevel.ToString(), myStyle);
```

What this line of code does is draw the `currentLevel` variable on our screen, between the two sets of buttons.

In the `Start()` function, add this line of code at the end:

```
myStyle.fontSize = 36;
```

We add this so that we can edit the size of the label font.

Creating an experience counter

The experience counter will show the player how much experience they earned as well as how much more experience is left until they gain a new level. To show this, we will use two GUI boxes: one for the player's current experience amount and the other for the total amount of experience possible.

First, we'll need to add a few variables; they'll be similar to the ones we used in the health bar:

```
public float maxExperience = 100;
public float currentExperience = 0;
public float currentExpBarLength;
public float maxExpBarLength = 100;
```

Our next step will be to draw it in the OnGUI() function:

```
currentExpBarLength = currentExperience * maxExpBarLength /
maxExperience;
if(currentExpBarLength > 5)
  GUI.Box(new Rect(Screen.width/2 - 20, Screen.height/2 - 300,
currentExpBarLength, 25), "");
  GUI.Box(new Rect(Screen.width/2 - 20, Screen.height/2 - 300,
maxExperience, 25), "");
```

As you can see, we follow the same code as we did to draw our health bar, except we draw two boxes on top of each other. The first box represents the current amount of experience; it only shows when the player has earned more than five experiences. This is to prevent the box from looking inside-out. The second box shows the maximum amount of experience.

Our next step will be to reset our experience and increase our level when the maximum amount of experience is gained. Enter this code:

```
if(currentExpBarLength >= maxExpBarLength)
{
  currentExpBarLength = 0;
  currentExperience = 0;
  currentLevel++;
}
```

In the preceding `if` statement, we check to see whether our current experience bar length is greater or equal to the maximum of the experience bar length. If it is, we reset our current experience and current experience bar length to `0`. Then, finally, we increase our current level. The 2D section of this chapter is now complete. This is what our scene looks like now with our 2D GUI:

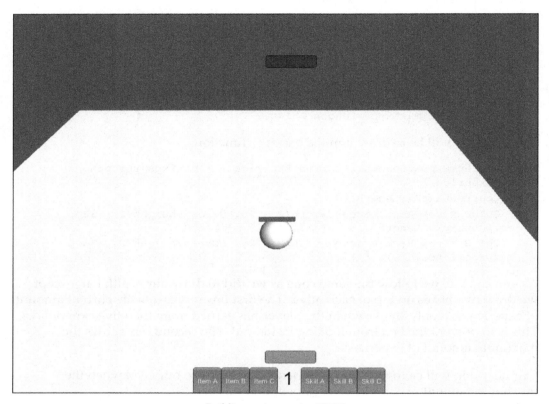

Building an immersive 3D UI

For our 3D GUI, we'll create similar elements that are used in 2D. We will create health bars, damage reports, and enemy name tags that will all appear to be in 3D.

Housing our 3D UI

We will follow similar steps when housing our 3D UI as we did when housing our 2D UI. Create a new script and call it `GUI_3D`.

Creating a 3D health bar

Our first step will be to add our variables needed for the health bar:

```
public float currentHealth = 100;
public float maximumHealth = 100;
float currentBarLength;
public Transform HealthBar;
Vector3 OrigScale;
```

The first three variables are what we'll use to calculate our health bar. The `Transform` variable is how we'll interact with our 3D object that's being used as our health bar. The `Vector3` variable is a reference point for when we scale the bar.

Our next step will be to add a `Start()` function. We'll use the `Start()` function to set the `OrigScale` variable:

```
void Start()
{
  OrigScale = HealthBar.transform.localScale;
}
```

We set `OrigScale` before we do anything else in the health bar. This is what we'll use as a reference point for the health bar. Next, we'll create our `Update()` function:

```
void Update()
{
  currentBarLength = currentHealth / maximumHealth;
  HealthBar.transform.LookAt(Camera.main.transform);

  if(Input.GetButton("Fire1"))
  {
    currentHealth -= 1.00f;
    ChangeBar();
  }
}
```

We will use `currentBarLength` to scale our object, so we set it by dividing `currentHealth` by `maximumHealth`. This will give us a value less than or equal to 1 and will scale our health bar perfectly. Next, we tell our `HealthBar` quad to look at our camera; this will allow us to always see it in 3D space. For testing purposes, we subtract the `currentHealth` value and call the `ChangeBar()` function when we press the left mouse button.

Our final step in creating the 3D health bar is to create the `ChangeBar()` function:

```
void ChangeBar()
{
  HealthBar.transform.localScale = Vector3.Lerp(OrigScale, new
Vector3(currentBarLength, OrigScale.y,OrigScale.z), Time.time);
}
```

Here, we set the `localScale` value of the `HealthBar` quad by lerping from `OrigScale` to our new scale. The new scale uses `CurrentBarLength` to determine the width of our health bar. When you press the left mouse button while testing the scene, you'll see the health bar go down over time.

Creating 3D damage reports

The damage reports will show up every time damage is done to our enemy. It'll pop up above the enemy for a brief amount of time and then disappear again. To start things off, we'll add a few variables to our script for the damage reports:

```
public TextMesh DamageReport;
public float Damage = 5;
Color txtColor;
public float SpawnTime = 2;
public float KillTime = 3;
public float PreviousTime = 0;
bool HasChanged = false;
```

The `TextMesh` object is the actual 3D text object that we use to show the damage report in-game. The `Damage` variable is what will be shown in the text of our `TextMesh`. We use a `Color` variable so that we can modify the alpha value of the `TextMesh` object; this will allow us to turn on/off the `TextMesh` object without having to instantiate it.

The next three float variables are used when we create a timer. We use the timer to pick when we want to show or hide the damage report. Lastly, the `bool` variable will help us check if we've taken damage or not.

Our next step will be to add a couple lines to our `Start()` function:

```
txtColor = DamageReport.color;
txtColor.a = 0;
```

The `txtColor` variable is what we'll use to show or hide the damage report. First, we set it to the color of `TextMesh`, and then we set its alpha value to zero. We set it to zero so that the player can only see it when damage is done.

The new Update function

Our next step is to add our `Update()` function. We will actually change this function a lot, so I'll show you the entire function and then go through it step by step:

```
void Update()
{
  currentBarLength = currentHealth / maximumHealth;
  HealthBar.transform.LookAt(Camera.main.transform);

  DamageReport.color = txtColor;
  if(Time.time > (SpawnTime + PreviousTime))
  {
    DamageReport.text = Damage.ToString();
    txtColor.a = 1;
    if(!HasChanged)
    {
      currentHealth -= Damage;
      ChangeBar();
    }
  }
  if(Time.time > (KillTime + PreviousTime))
  {
    DamageReport.text = "";

    txtColor.a = 0;
    PreviousTime = Time.time;
    HasChanged = false;
  }
}
```

The first two lines of the function haven't changed, but they should remain at the top of the function. The next line sets the color of our `TextMesh` to our color variable. Now we will encounter our first timer:

```
if(Time.time > (SpawnTime + PreviousTime))
{
  DamageReport.text = Damage.ToString();
  txtColor.a = 1;
  if(!HasChanged)
  {
    currentHealth -= Damage;
    ChangeBar();
  }
}
```

Here, we check whether the current time passed in-game is greater than the value of the `SpawnTime` variable plus the `PreviousTime` variable. `SpawnTime` is the variable that we use to spawn the damage report. `PreviousTime` will be set later; this is used to mark the previous time we showed the damage report.

When the current time passed is greater than `SpawnTime` and `PreviousTime` together, we show the damage report. We first set the text of `TextMesh` to the value of the damage variable. Then, we set its alpha value to one; this is so that the player can see it on the screen.

Afterwards, we check whether `HasChanged` is false. If it is false, then we subtract the health with our `Damage` variable. We then run the `ChangeBar` function. Time to look at the next timer:

```
if(Time.time > (KillTime + PreviousTime))
{
  DamageReport.text = "";

  txtColor.a = 0;
  PreviousTime = Time.time;
  HasChanged = false;
}
```

The `if` statement is similar to the previous timer, but we check with `KillTime` instead of `SpawnTime`. `KillTime` is what we'll use to hide the damage report. Within the `if` statement in the first line, we set the text of `TextMesh` to an empty value. For good measure, we set the alpha value of `TextMesh` to zero to hide it.

After this, we set the `PreviousTime` variable to the current time passed in-game. This will represent the last time damage report in the game. Finally, we set the `HasChanged` variable to false.

Completing the damage reports

Our last step in creating the damage report will be to add one line of code to the `ChangeBar()` function:

```
HasChanged = true;
```

Setting this to `true` will allow us to run the `ChangeBar()` function again. We use the `bool` variable so that the `ChangeBar()` function doesn't continually run in the `Update()` function. If we didn't use the `bool` variable, our `currentHealth` would run down past zero and the scale of our health bar would be in the negative.

Creating 3D name tags

The name tag is what will be used to show the player what the enemy's name and level is. To create it, we'll perform similar steps as we did while creating the damage reports. Our first step is to add a few variables:

```
public string Name = "Skeleton Warrior";
public int Level = 1;
public TextMesh NameTag;
```

We set all our variables here to `public` so that we can access them later. The `Name` string is the enemy's name, the `Level` integer is the enemy's level, and `TextMesh NameTag` is the object we use to represent the previous two variables.

Next, we will create a new function, which we will use to set the name tag. Add this function to the bottom of your script:

```
void SetNameTag()
{
   NameTag.text = Level + "    " + Name;
}
```

Here, we set the `NameTag` text to the level and name variables. We add a few spaces between them so that the name tag looks good on the screen. This completes the creation of our name tag as well as our 3D GUI. Here's what our scene now looks like with our 2D and 3D GUI:

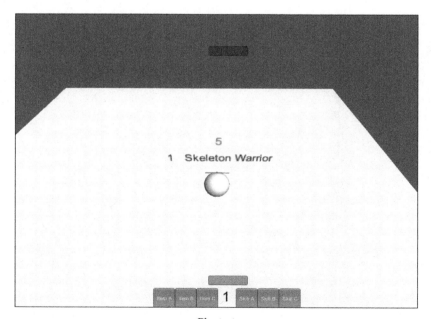

Playtest

Try these steps to playtest the different parts of this chapter:

1. Press the play button and test to see if everything works correctly.

2. Move the camera around to different angles to ensure the 3D GUI always looks at the camera.

3. To test the GUI buttons, add the `Debug.Log` statements to them to show that they work.

4. Iterate the `currentExperience` variable to ensure the experience bar works correctly.

5. Modify the timer variables to see which fits better.

Summary

In this chapter, you learned a few ways to create a GUI. First, you started off by learning the traditional way of creating the GUI by making buttons, bars, and text. Then, we switched gears and learned how to make a 3D GUI by making 3D health bars, 3D damage reports, and 3D name tags.

In the next chapter, you will learn how to make a few different classes for in-game items. First, we'll create a class so that items will affect the player, the next class will allow items to affect other objects on touch, and the final class will be created for projectiles. All of these can be used for the player, enemies, or environment objects.

Expandable Item Classes

3

Items in video games are very important. They can be tools, weapons, healing items, traps, clothing, armor, ammo, keys, and so on. Items are what the player will interact with the most in your game. Since the items are so often used, it is a good practice to create item classes that can be expanded and used in all possible situations without having to rewrite the class.

In this chapter, we will cover the following topics:

- Creating customizable classes for items
- Learning how GameObjects can interact with each other through sending messages
- Creating an `Item` class that affects the player
- Creating a `Melee` item class that will affect environments and enemies
- Creating a `Projectile` item class that can be used for items that travel distances
- Utilizing a classification system for all objects to decide what they do
- Using trigger-based collisions for the `Melee` and `Projectile` item classes
- Using two types of movement for projectile items

The self item class

The first item class we'll create is for an item that affects the player upon usage. Items that players use typically affects their various stats either by adding or removing them or buffing/debuffing them for a certain amount of time. Now let's start scripting; create a new script and name it `itemSelf`.

Adding our variables

Our first set of variables will actually be added outside of our class as they are enum variables:

```
public enum SelfAction {BuffDebuff, ChangeHP, ChangeArmor, None};
public enum SelfType {Armor, Potion, None};
```

The first enum we created will be used to pick what the item does. We've got a few options for our items, but this can be expanded and customized to your liking. The second enum we use will determine of what type the item is; for now, we're just checking to see whether it's a potion or armor. Now let's add the rest of our variables:

```
public GameObject Player;
public int Amount, Value, ArmorAmount;
public float Weight;
public string Name, Stat;
public SelfAction selfAction = SelfAction.None;
public SelfType selfType = SelfType.None;
```

We add a GameObject so that we have a player reference to adjust stats. The rest of the variables we added are for the item stats. Finally, we add our two enums to our list of variables. We make these variables public so that anyone can just drag-and-drop the scripts for easy item creation.

Buff or debuff stats

The first function we'll add to our item script will allow us to add or subtract player stats. Add the following code to your script:

```
void BuffDebuffStat()
{
   Player.SendMessage("BuffDebuffStat", new KeyValuePair<string,
int>(Stat, Amount));
}
```

When we call this function, we send a message to our player, which will call a function in a script on the player that will add or subtract the stat we specify. In this message, we tell this function which function to call as well as send a `KeyValuePair` variable. We use a `KeyValuePair` variable to send both the stat we want to modify as well as the amount that we want to modify it by.

The health changer

Our next function to be added will be one that will affect the player's health. Add the following code to your script:

```
void ChangeHealth()
{
    Player.SendMessage("ChangeHealth", Amount);
}
```

When we call `ChangeHealth`, we send a message to the player to call a function known as `ChangeHealth`, and we send `Amount` as well. As you can see, we use `Amount` often. Since changing stats is all about amounts, we use a single variable to make it easier for us.

The armor changer

The next and final stat modifying function we'll add will allow us to adjust the armor of our player. Add this function to your script:

```
void ChangeArmorAmount()
{
    Player.SendMessage("ChangeArmorAmount", ArmorAmount);
}
```

This function is similar to the `ChangeHealth` function. We send the player a message to call a function that will change the player's armor amount. Then, we also send it the amount we want to change it by.

The item activator

This last function that we add will be called by other classes to activate the item. Add this last function to your script:

```
void Activate()
{
    switch(selfAction)
    {
    case SelfAction.BuffDebuff:
        BuffDebuffStat();
        break;
    case SelfAction.ChangeHP:
        ChangeHealth();
```

```
      break;
  case SelfAction.ChangeArmor:
    ChangeArmorAmount();
    break;
  }

  if(selfType == SelfType.Potion)
    Destroy(gameObject);
}
```

When this function is called, we use a `switch` statement to check the `selfAction` variable. This is an easy way to see what the item should do when the player uses it. At the end of the `Activate` function, we check to see what type of item it is. If it is a potion, we destroy the GameObject. Not all items get destroyed upon use, such as armor, so we use the `selfType` variable to determine what type of item it is.

The melee item class

The melee item class will have similar properties and functions as the self item class. What is different about the two is that the functions don't affect the player, but other GameObjects. Also, the way we activate the item is different.

To get started, create a new script and name it `itemMelee`. We'll start our script by adding some variables, similar to the ones we used in the `itemSelf` class.

Adding our variables

First, we'll add a couple of enum variables:

```
public enum MeleeAction {BuffDebuff, ChangeHP, ActivateEnv, None};
public enum MeleeType {Weapon, Potion, None};
```

The `MeleeAction` enum will decide what the melee item does. Since melee items can interact with various GameObjects, its actions will vary just as much as it can. The `MeleeType` enum will determine whether the player uses a weapon, potion, or no items. Now, let's add the rest of our variables in:

```
public int Amount, Value;
public float Weight;
public string Name, Stat;
public MeleeAction meleeAction = MeleeAction.None;
public MeleeType meleeType = MeleeType.None;
```

As you can see, the variables are similar to the ones we used in our `itemSelf` class; our only major differences are the different names for our `Type` and `Action` enums.

Buff or debuff stats

The first function that we'll add to our melee item will allow melee items to modify the stats of other objects. Add this function to the script:

```
void BuffDebuffStat(GameObject other)
{
  other.SendMessage("BuffDebuffStat", new KeyValuePair<string,
int>(Stat, Amount));
}
```

This function, when called, receives a GameObject, which will be the GameObject that we are affecting with the melee item. We then send a message to that GameObject to call the function that modifies the stats, and then pass the KeyValuePair to it. The KeyValuePair contains the stat we want to modify as well as the amount that we want to modify it by.

The health changer

The next function we'll add to the script will allow the melee item to change the health of other GameObjects. Add the following function after the BuffDebuffStat function in our script:

```
void ChangeHealth(GameObject other)
{
  other.SendMessage("ChangeHealth", Amount);
}
```

When this function is called, it will modify the health of the GameObject that the melee item collides with. This could mean healing or hurting the GameObject, but this function can be used either way.

Let's interact with the environment

The last and final function will allow the player to interact with the environment. Add this function to your script:

```
void ActivateEnvironment(GameObject other)
{
  other.SendMessage("Activate");
}
```

This function is called when the melee item collides with an environmental object the player can interact with. We send the object we want to interact with the message to activate. From here, the other GameObject handles the rest of the interaction.

Detecting triggers

In order to call the functions that we just created, we have to create the interaction between the melee item and the other GameObject. Add this final function to the script:

```
void OnTriggerEnter(Collider col)
{
  switch(col.gameObject.tag)
  {
  case "Enemy":
    if(meleeType != MeleeType.Potion)
    {
      if(meleeAction == MeleeAction.ChangeHP)
        ChangeHealth(col.gameObject);

      if(meleeAction == MeleeAction.BuffDebuff)
        BuffDebuffStat(col.gameObject);

      if(meleeAction == MeleeAction.ActivateEnv)
        ActivateEnvironment(col.gameObject);
    }
    break;
  case "Environment":
    if(meleeType == MeleeType.Potion)
    {
      if(meleeAction == MeleeAction.ChangeHP)
        ChangeHealth(col.gameObject);

      if(meleeAction == MeleeAction.BuffDebuff)
        BuffDebuffStat(col.gameObject);
    }
    break;
  }

  if(meleeType == MeleeType.Potion)
    Destroy(gameObject);
}
```

To detect the contact between the melee item and GameObject that the player hits, we use `OnTriggerEnter` to activate our functions. When the melee item enters a triggered GameObject, the `OnTriggerEnter` function is called and it will receive the GameObject that it entered.

From here, we use a `switch` statement to check the tag of the trigger GameObject. Using a tag is a quick way to check what the player hit with their melee item. Once we find the correctly tagged GameObject, we check the `meleeType` variable and then the `meleeAction` variable.

Depending on the type of melee item, we decide what the item can and can't do. In both `case` statements, we check whether the melee type is a potion or not; this will decide whether to activate environmental objects or not. Also, at the end of the function, we destroy the melee item if it is a potion; this ensures that potions are a single-use item.

The projectile item class

It is time for our final item class, which is the projectile item class. These kinds of items could be bullets, arrows, thrown items, and so on. The projectile item class will be similar to the melee item class, except this one will have functions that will allow it to move in the game world. We'll start by creating a new script and naming it `itemRanged`.

Adding our variables

As we did in the previous two classes, we'll need to first add a few enums to our script. Add these variables to our script:

```
public enum RangedAction {BuffDebuff, ChangeHP, ActivateEnv, None};
public enum RangedType {Weapon, None};
public enum MovementType {Basic, Drop, None};
```

You can see that we have a couple of familiar variables that we will use for the action and type of the item. We also have a new enum; this one will be used to determine how the object will move when it's created. The basic type will move the object through the air with simple movement. The drop type is similar to the basic type, but will allow the object to drop in the air as if gravity was acting on it.

Now, let's add the rest of our variables:

```
public int Amount, Value;
public float Weight, Speed, DropSpeed;
public string Name, Stat;
public RangedAction rangedAction = RangedAction.None;
public RangedType rangedType = RangedType.None;
public MovementType moveType = MovementType.None;
```

As you can tell, many of these variables are similar to the ones we previously used. These variables are typical to our items; the only one that is different is the `MovementType` enum. Now let's move on to adding our functions.

Buff or debuff stats

Let's allow our projectile to affect enemy stats; add this function to our script:

```
void BuffDebuffStat(GameObject other)
{
  other.SendMessage("BuffDebuffStat", new KeyValuePair<string,
int>(Stat, Amount));
}
```

Just like the melee item, we receive the GameObject that the projectile collides with. Then, we send a message to that object to call a function and send it a `KeyValuePair` variable.

The health changer

Our next function will allow our projectile to do the most common effect that projectiles have, which is hurt or heal others. Let's add the following function to our script:

```
void ChangeHealth(GameObject other)
{
  other.SendMessage("ChangeHealth", Amount);
}
```

This function should be familiar; it acts the same way as the one we used in the melee item.

Adding movement

These next few functions will add movement to our projectile. We have two kinds of movements, so we'll separate them into two different functions:

```
void BasicMovement()
{
  transform.Translate(Vector3.forward * (Time.deltaTime * Speed));
}

void DropMovement()
{
  transform.Translate(new Vector3(0, DropSpeed, 1) * (Time.deltaTime *
Speed));
```

```
    }

    void Update()
    {
      switch(moveType)
      {
      case MovementType.Basic:
        BasicMovement();
        break;
      case MovementType.Drop:
        DropMovement();
        break;
      }
    }
```

In the `Update` function, we check the `moveType` variable in a `switch` statement to determine how the projectile will move through the air. Depending on the value you assign to it, it'll either call the `BasicMovement` function or the `DropMovement` function. Let's take a look at the `BasicMovement` code:

```
    transform.Translate(Vector3.forward * (Time.deltaTime * Speed));
```

Here we set the transform of the GameObject to move forward in the *z* axis. We multiply the movement `Vector` by `deltaTime` and our `Speed` variable. The `Speed` variable will allow you to control how fast or slow the projectile will go:

Now let's take a look at the `DropMovement` code:

```
    transform.Translate(new Vector3(0, DropSpeed, 1) * (Time.deltaTime *
    Speed));
```

This line is similar to the `BasicMovement` line, but our movement `Vector` is different. We use the `DropSpeed` variable in the *y* axis to make our projectile drop to the ground. It will appear as if gravity is acting on our projectile, giving it a more realistic appearance. Dropping the projectile will also make it a little more difficult for the player to attack, adding a new mechanic to the game.

Detecting triggers

Now we'll add detection method to our projectile. We will use a similar system that we used in the melee item class. Add the following code to your script:

```
    void OnTriggerEnter(Collider col)
    {
      switch(col.gameObject.tag)
      {
```

```
      case "Enemy":
        if(rangedType == RangedType.Weapon)
        {
          if(rangedType != RangedType.None)
          {
            if(rangedAction == RangedAction.ChangeHP)
              ChangeHealth(col.gameObject);

            if(rangedAction == RangedAction.BuffDebuff)
              BuffDebuffStat(col.gameObject);

            if(rangedAction == RangedAction.ActivateEnv)
              ActivateEnvironment(col.gameObject);
          }
        }
        break;
      case "Environment":
        if(rangedType != RangedType.None)
        {
          if(rangedAction == RangedAction.ChangeHP)
            ChangeHealth(col.gameObject);

          if(rangedAction == RangedAction.BuffDebuff)
            BuffDebuffStat(col.gameObject);

          if(rangedAction == RangedAction.ActivateEnv)
            ActivateEnvironment(col.gameObject);
        }
        break;
    }
    Destroy(gameObject);
}
```

Just as in the melee item class, we use triggers to detect whether the projectile has hit something; if it does, we take the collider of that GameObject. Once we have detected the collision and received the collider, we follow these steps to decide what to do next:

- In the `switch` statement, we use the tag of the GameObject collider to check what it's colliding with
- We then check if the `rangedType` variable isn't equal to `None`
- Afterwards, we go through a few `if` statements to see what action we are using
- Once the action has been found, we call its function accordingly
- While calling the function, we pass the GameObject as well
- Finally, after all this is done, we delete the projectile from the scene

At first, it may look confusing, but we are really just following a step-by-step process of logic to decide what our projectile should do. With this, we conclude the projectile item class as well as all of our item classes we created. Next, we move on to playtesting!

Playtesting

To playtest these item classes, try doing any of the following:

- Keep in mind that to use triggers, your GameObject must be a RigidBody
- Modify all of the variables to see what different results you get
- Try different combinations of actions and types to see what happens
- Add more actions and types to the classes and see how your functions behave for them
- Set up a test scene and use all of the item classes we created
- Modify the speed variables in the projectile class to see the varying results
- For melee items, add a `health` variable to it and create an endurance system
- For projectile items, see if you can figure out how to allow the item to pass though multiple objects before destroying itself
- For self items, try to add a functionality to allow multiple uses of items before they get destroyed

Summary

In this chapter, you learned how to create three different kinds of items. First, we created a class of items that would affect the player upon activation. Then, we delved into a class for melee items that affect other GameObjects. Finally, we created a class for projectile items. All of these classes have similar properties and methods, yet each one is used slightly different each time.

In the next chapter, we will go over how to create an inventory system. First, we will figure out how to make a storage system that fits our game. Next, we'll create a GUI-based interface system so that the player can interact with their inventory easily. Finally, we'll create a *Quick Equip* system. This will allow the player to equip or use various items by using hot keys either on the screen, on their keyboard, or on their controller without pausing to go to the inventory menu.

4
Inventory

In this chapter, we will create an inventory storage system. We'll also create a GUI representation of the inventory for the player to interact with, as well as showing the player their quick items. Items that can be quickly used or equipped using easy access keys are known as quick items; they are used frequently in RPG and FPS games. Inventories are used in many games from all genres, so having a good way to make one is very helpful.

In this chapter, we will cover the following topics:

- Creating a storage system for GameObjects
- Adding items to the inventory
- Removing items from the inventory
- Initializing the inventory
- Setting the inventory size to be dynamic
- Making it possible to have multiples of items
- Setting quick items that can be used by our custom quick item inputs
- Accessing the inventory using our custom inventory inputs
- Displaying the inventory on screen via GUI

Features of an inventory

Before creating an inventory, you must figure out what kind of inventory fits your game best. There are various features that an inventory has that will need to be figured out when designing one. The following are the features that we will discuss:

- Limits
- Accessibility
- Order

Limits of the inventory

There are two common ways to limit an inventory; they are weight and slot size. If an inventory is based on weight, it will only carry a certain number of objects that are within its weight bearing limits. If an inventory is based on slot size, the player can have as many objects as long as there are slots and the weight of an object either doesn't matter or isn't tracked at all.

An example of a weight-limited inventory is found in games such as **The Elder Scrolls V: Skyrim**. The player can keep items in their inventory up to a certain accumulated weight limit. An example of a slot size limited inventory is found in games such as **Borderlands**. In Borderlands, the player's backpack is set to a certain number of slots where they can keep items; if the limit is reached, the player can't pick up any more items.

There is a third way to limit inventory, which is to combine the slot size method with the weight method. An example of this combination method is **Baldur's Gate 2**. In this game, the player has a backpack with multiple slots, but also a weight limit. So they may at times reach the weight limit in the inventory, but still have slots open in the inventory. Alternatively, they can reach the slot size limit of the inventory but still be holding less than the maximum weight limit.

Accessing the inventory

To access the inventory, you, as the designer, have a few options to choose from. Some of the more common ways to allow the player to access the inventory are a menu system, quick-items, and an item bar. You can also combine any or all of these methods to allow to the player to utilize the inventory in dynamic ways.

In a menu-based inventory, when the player presses a key on their keyboard or a button on their gamepad, they are taken out of the gameplay to the inventory menu. Depending on the game, this can be a single menu showing their entire inventory, or a menu broken up into submenus to organize their items.

When a quick-item method is used to access the inventory, the player just presses a key or button and their item is instantly selected. For some games, this item might need to be assigned first in an inventory menu, or in some games it may be predefined as to which item is assigned to which key or button.

If you create a game where the player will need to use a lot of items and you don't want them to open a menu stop the gameplay, then an item bar might be what you need. An example of an item bar can be seen in **Massive Multiplayer Online** games such as **World of Warcraft**. This is where the player has a GUI-based bar with button slots to hold items, spells, abilities, and so on. What each of the buttons does can be customized by the player so that they can get full control over and access to their favorite or most used items without having to use a menu to access them.

Organizing an inventory

The items within an inventory can be organized in a few ways depending on the physical size, item type, slot size, or alphabetical order. Organization by physical size can be either lightest to heaviest or heaviest to lightest. When organizing by item type, healing items should be kept separate from weapons and armor. These separate item types can be split up into multiple submenus: one each for weapons, armor, healing items, and so on.

Organization by slot size can be seen in games such as the *Diablo* series, where the items vary in slot size both vertically and horizontally. The player must move items around in their inventory to make room for other items. The last method of organizing items in the inventory, as mentioned previously, is alphabetically. This will show items by names from the beginning of the alphabet or from the end.

Item count modifications

Now that we have discussed the features of the inventory, we need to figure out how items in the inventory can be gained or lost. This can be done in the following ways:

- Buying, selling, and trading items
- Dropping and picking up items
- Destroying or using items

Item bartering

If your game has a lot of items in its world, you might have included shops within that world. In these shops, the player can sell their items or buy more items. This method is very common in role-playing games, as these types of games have many items. Another way to barter items is to trade them. This can be done in offline games, but this is mostly seen in online games where players can use a menu system to trade their items.

Dropping and picking up items

When the player's inventory is full or almost full, they might come across an item that they want. If the option is made available, the player can drop an item they don't want anymore and pick up the new item to replace it. Dropping an item can insert it back in the game world or simply destroy it. Picking up an item can be done by walking over it or selecting it with a key or button.

Destroying and using items

If the player has a bow, they will most likely have a multitude of arrows to shoot. When these arrows are shot, the number of arrows will go down. Once all arrows have been shot, the arrows will no longer be in their inventory, since the player has used them all. Using healing items might also modify how many healing items are left, unless the items are designed to stay in the inventory without a limit on usage.

Destroying an item can be done manually by the player if they no longer want to keep that item. There can also be a condition stat on a weapon or a piece of armor. When the condition gets too low, the item will be destroyed in the inventory, making it unusable. Another way to destroy an item is to assign it a certain number of uses; once it exceeds this number of uses, it can be destroyed automatically.

Displaying the inventory

The final step in using an inventory is to display it to the player. This is done on the GUI with icons, images, or with the 3D model. The icon can either be a scaled down image of the item, or it can be a silhouette of the item to represent it. An example showing the 3D model of the item can be seen in *The Elder Scrolls V: Skyrim*, where the player can select the item in their inventory and interact with the 3D model to look at it.

Creating the inventory script

For our inventory, we'll only use one script, so let's get it started.

Creating and naming the script

The first thing we need to do is to create a new C# script and name it Inventory. When you open the script, delete the Start and Update functions, leaving an empty class for us to use.

Adding the necessary variables

First, add this `using` statement where the other `using` statements are. The `using` statement will be needed so that we can use the `List` container variable:

```
using System.Collections.Generic;
```

Now, let's add the variables we require and place them after the opening class defining bracket:

```
bool showInventory = false;
public Rect inventoryRect = new Rect(Screen.width / 2, Screen.height /
2, 400, 400);
public GameObject EmptyObject;
public int InventorySize = 9;
public GameObject[] invItems;
public GameObject[] QuickItems;

List<KeyValuePair<int, GameObject>> items = new List<KeyValuePair<int,
GameObject>>();

List<KeyValuePair<int, int>> itemCount = new List<KeyValuePair<int,
int>>();
```

The `showInventory` variable will be used when we activate an input. This is how we determine when to and when not to show the inventory GUI. Next, we have a `Rectangle` variable, that we'll use to determine where we put the inventory GUI and what size it should be. By default, we set the **X** and **Y** positions to the center of the screen.

Our next variable is a GameObject; in the **Inspector** panel we will set this as an empty object. We'll be using the empty object in our inventory as a placeholder when there is no item to be placed there. The next variable, aptly named `InventorySize`, will determine the size of our inventory.

The next two variables are GameObject arrays. We use these to hold the actual GameObject items that we will hold in our Inventory. `InvItems` will hold the GameObjects that are in our inventory and `QuickItems` will hold the GameObjects that the player wants as their quick-items.

Lastly, we have two lists for our final variables. The first one will hold the GameObject items within our inventory; the list is made up of `KeyValuePairs`. The key will be the ID of our item and the value is a GameObject, which is the item in our inventory.

Our next list is also made up of `KeyValuePairs` and both the `Key` and `Value` are integers. The `Key` will be our ID that will match `itemCount` to the correct inventory item. The `Value` will be the actual number of items that we have.

Initializing our inventory

Time for our first function! This method will be used to create our inventory for the first time.

Creating the initializer

Let's create our initializer by adding the following function to the script:

```
void InitializeInventory()
{
  invItems = new GameObject[InventorySize];
  for(int i = 0; i < InventorySize; i++)
  {
    invItems[i] = EmptyObject;
    items.Add(new KeyValuePair<int, GameObject>(i, invItems[i]));
    itemCount.Add(new KeyValuePair<int, int>(i, 0));

    if(i < QuickItems.Length)
      QuickItems[i] = invItems[i];
  }
}
```

The first line within the new function sets the `invItems` array size to the `InventorySize` variable. Next, we have a `for` loop that will initialize the inventory. First, it sets each `invItem` value to our `EmptyObject` GameObject variable, which is our placeholder until we start adding items to the inventory.

Next, we add a new `KeyValuePair` variable to each slot within the items list. The key of the new `KeyValuePair` variable will be our iterator variable from the `for` loop. The value of the new `KeyValuePair` variable will be the GameObject within the `invItems` array that currently holds the spot that our iterator is valued at. This is so that the `invItems` array and items list are ordered in the same way.

After this, we add a new `KeyValuePair` variable to our `itemCount` list. The key is going to be set to our iterator variable as well and the value will be set to 0. This will ensure that every item in our inventory will have no value assigned to it, until we start adding items.

The last two lines in our `for` loop will create our default quick items. We use an `if` statement to check whether the value of our iterator is still less than the length of our `QuickItems` array. If it is, we set each `QuickItems` in the array to what is in our `invItems` array, which is our `EmptyObject` GameObject. To call this function, we'll put it within an `Awake` function, as follows:

```
void Awake()
{
   InitializeInventory();
}
```

We have created our inventory. It's currently an empty inventory, but all the necessary containers have been created and assigned to default values. Since we used an iterator variable for all the keys and arrays, all the values in the containers coincide with each other. We also created and assigned our quick items to empty GameObjects, just as we did for our inventory.

Adding items

Now, we'll create our first interaction with the inventory: adding items. This is probably the most important aspect of having an inventory. Why have an inventory that can't have items added to it?

Let's figure this out

Before we jump into the coding, let's take a moment and plan out how we want to add items to our inventory. From the player's point of view, adding items to their inventory is something as simple as placing the item in their bag, or walking into the object and having it appear in their inventory. What they do is similar to how we will add items. They see an empty slot in their inventory and then place their newly obtained item into that slot. We will be following a process similar to that within our code, creating an inventory system that allows the player to pick up items off the ground.

Creating the adding function

Add the following function to your script, just below the `InitializeInventory` function:

```
void AddToInventory(int HowMany, GameObject NewItem)
{
   for(int i = 0; i < invItems.Length; i++)
   {
```

```
      if(invItems[i].name != "Empty")
      {
        if(invItems[i].name == NewItem.name)
        {
          int val = itemCount[i].Value + HowMany;
          itemCount[i] = new KeyValuePair<int, int>(itemCount[i].Key,
  val);
        break
        };
      }
      else
      {
        int val = itemCount[i].Value + HowMany;
        invItems[i] = NewItem;
        items.Add(new KeyValuePair<int, GameObject>(i, NewItem));
        itemCount.Add(new KeyValuePair<int, int>(i, val));
        break;
      }
    }
  }
```

The first thing you'll notice is that our function takes in two variables, an `int` and a `GameObject` variables. The `int` variable is the number of new items that we want to add to the inventory. The GameObject is the new item that we want to add to the inventory. Now, let's go over how exactly we are going to add items to the inventory.

We use a `for` loop to iterate through each item of our `invItems` array, since this is the array that is holding our inventory items. First, we check whether the name of current `invItem` is not empty. The only object that we'll be using with the name `"Empty"` is actually our `EmptyObject` variable, which is our placeholder object.

So if the current `invItem` isn't empty, we move on to check whether its name is equal to that of the new item's name. If it is, we create a new `int` variable named `val`. The `val` integer is assigned the total of the current `invItem` variable's value and the value of the new item we want to add. After we do this, we set the current `itemCount` value to `val` by assigning it a new `KeyValuePair` variable. The key is the current `itemCount` ID and the value is its amount. After this, we stop the `for` loop with `break`, so that we no longer iterate through our inventory.

If the current `invItem` variable is empty, we add the new GameObject to our inventory. We do this by creating the same `val` integer as we did recently for our amount, and assigning the value of the current `itemCount` value plus the amount of the item that we want to add. Then, we assign current `invItems` GameObject to `NewItem`, the GameObject passed into the function.

Next, we add the new item to our items list by creating a new `KeyValuePair` variable and assigning its key to the iterator and its value to `NewItem`. Finally, we add the new item's amount by adding it to the `itemCount` list. This is done by creating another new `KeyValuePair` variable. We assign the new `KeyValuePair` variable's key to the iterator and its value to the `val` variable.

With this, you now have the capability to add new items to your inventory. When adding the items, you can add as many as you want. If you want only one of the new items in the inventory, just set `HowMany` to `1`, and if you want to remove one, set it to `-1`.

Removing items

Now, we'll add the second most important aspect of inventories, removing items! This is handy for those times when a player uses their health potion, sells an item, shoots a rocket, or drops their coins!

Let's figure this out

Just like we did when we added items, let's take a moment to think about how we want to remove items from the inventory. Again, from the player's point of view, how is this done? Well when they sell the item, they are selecting the item personally. If the player shoots their gun or bow, their ammo is dispensed immediately. When the player meets their untimely death, their items may be dropped on the ground or left on their corpse to be looted by their assailant. During the selling item phase and shooting gun action, they pick what item they want to get rid of from their inventory. We will follow a similar process when removing items from the inventory.

Creating the removing function

Add the following function to the script, just below the `AddToInventory` function:

```
void RemoveFromInventory(int HowMany, GameObject Item)
{
  for(int i = 0; i < items.Capacity; i++)
  {
    if(invItems[i].name != "Empty")
    {
      if(invItems[i].name == Item.name)
      {
        int val = itemCount[i].Value - HowMany;
        itemCount[i] = new KeyValuePair<int, int>(itemCount[i].Key,
val);
```

```
            if(itemCount[i].Value <= 0)
            {
                invItems[i] = EmptyObject;
                items[i] = new KeyValuePair<int, GameObject>(i,
    EmptyObject);
                itemCount[i] = new KeyValuePair<int, int>(itemCount[i].Key,
    0);
            }
            break;
        }
      }
    }
}
```

Just as when we added items to the inventory, we pass an int variable and a GameObject to this function. The int variable is the number of the items we want to remove, and the GameObject is the actual item that we want to remove. Now we iterate through the items array, which is the array holding our inventory of items.

First we check whether the current invItem variable's name isn't "Empty". If it isn't, then we move on to see whether the name of the current invItem variable is equal to the name of the item we want to remove from the inventory. Similar to how we added items to the inventory, we'll need to create a new int variable, which will hold the value of the item that we'll decrease. This time, val will be equal to the current itemCount value subtracted from the HowMany integer that was passed into the function. We then assign the current itemCount variable a new KeyValuePair variable, using the same key as key and using val as the value.

Now, we do something a little different from what we did while adding items. We check whether the current itemCount value is less than or equal to zero; if it is, we have to do a few things. When an item has an amount of zero or less we have to remove it from the inventory.

Our first step to remove the item from the inventory will be to set the current invItem value to our EmptyObject variable, the placeholder. Next, we set the current item's KeyValuePair variable to new KeyValuePair, the new KeyValuePair variable will have the iterator as the key and the EmptyObject GameObject as its value. Finally, we set the current itemCount KeyValuePair to a new KeyValuePair as well. Its key will stay the same, but we set the value to 0.

After this is all done, we stop the loop with break. Remember when we checked whether the current invItems name was equal to "Empty"? If it does happen to be "Empty", we use break again to stop the loop. We can't remove the item from the inventory, since it is in the inventory to begin with!

With that, you now have the ability to remove items from the inventory. When the player sells an item, shoots an arrow, use a health potion, or anything similar to these situations, you can remove that specific item from the inventory. This may seem like a daunting task, but there is a way around this. You can also use the `InitializeInventory` function that we first created to reset the inventory, since that is essentially what that function does.

Setting the quick-select items

In many games, there is a mechanism known as quick-items or quick-select items. These are items that the player uses often and wants to have access to very quickly without having to stop the game to go into their inventory. They are typically accessed by the number keys on the keyboard or the directional pad on a controller. We will add a small function into our inventory that will allow us to assign quick-items.

Setting the quick-select items quickly

Add this function to your script, under the `RemoveFromInventory` function:

```
void SetQuickItem(GameObject NewItem, int QuickInput)
{
    if(QuickItems[QuickInput].name != NewItem.name)
        if(QuickInput < QuickItems.Length)
            QuickItems[QuickInput] = NewItem;
}
```

This function takes in two variables, the GameObject that we want as the quick-item and the slot that we want to assign it to. In the actual function, we check whether the name of the GameObject in the current `QuickItems` array is the same as the name of `NewItem`. If it is not same, then we will not do anything because the item is already in that quick-item slot. If it isn't, then we assign the `QuickItems` array slot, which is `QuickInput`, to the GameObject passed into the function.

Let's display the inventory

Now let's move on to the next important aspect of the inventory, showing it to the player! To do this, we will use `GUILayout` and a GUI window.

Using our custom inputs

To access the inventory, we have set up a couple of inputs for our player to use to view the inventory. Let's add an `Update` function along with some code that will show the inventory:

```
void Update()
{
   if(Input.GetButtonUp("I_Key") || Input.GetButtonUp("A_360"))
   {
      showInventory = (showInventory) ? false : true;
   }
}
```

In the `Update` function, we check whether the `"I_Key"` or `"A_360"` inputs are pressed. When one of the inputs is pressed, we switch the `showInventory` Boolean. When the `showInventory` Boolean is `true`, we show the inventory GUI to the player; if it is `false`, then we hide the inventory GUI.

Displaying the GUI

Now let's add the `OnGUI` function to the script, just below the `Update` function:

```
void OnGUI()
{
   if(showInventory)
   {
      inventoryRect = GUI.Window(0, inventoryRect, InventoryGUI,
"Inventory");
   }
}
```

When the `showInventory` Boolean is `true`, we show the inventory GUI. We do this by setting our `inventoryRect` rectangle variable to a GUI window. The GUI window will show the inventory window, as well as give it the title `"Inventory"`.

Running the GUI

Now, to run the window, we need a function that will show the contents of the GUI window. Add the following function to your script, under the `OnGUI` function:

```
void InventoryGUI(int ID)
{
   GUILayout.BeginArea(new Rect(0, 50, 400, 350));
```

```
    GUILayout.BeginHorizontal();
    GUILayout.Button(itemCount[0].Value.ToString() + " " + invItems[0].
name, GUILayout.Height(75));
    GUILayout.Button(itemCount[1].Value.ToString() + " " + invItems[1].
name, GUILayout.Height(75));
    GUILayout.Button(itemCount[2].Value.ToString() + " " + invItems[2].
name, GUILayout.Height(75));
    GUILayout.EndHorizontal();

    GUILayout.BeginHorizontal();
    GUILayout.Button(itemCount[3].Value.ToString() + " " + invItems[3].
name, GUILayout.Height(75));
    GUILayout.Button(itemCount[4].Value.ToString() + " " + invItems[4].
name, GUILayout.Height(75));
    GUILayout.Button(itemCount[5].Value.ToString() + " " + invItems[5].
name, GUILayout.Height(75));
    GUILayout.EndHorizontal();

    GUILayout.BeginHorizontal();
    GUILayout.Button(itemCount[6].Value.ToString() + " " + invItems[6].
name, GUILayout.Height(75));
    GUILayout.Button(itemCount[7].Value.ToString() + " " + invItems[7].
name, GUILayout.Height(75));
    GUILayout.Button(itemCount[8].Value.ToString() + " " + invItems[8].
name, GUILayout.Height(75));
    GUILayout.EndHorizontal();

    GUILayout.BeginHorizontal();
    GUILayout.Button(QuickItems[0].name, GUILayout.Height(50));
    GUILayout.Button(QuickItems[1].name, GUILayout.Height(50));
    GUILayout.EndHorizontal();

    GUILayout.BeginHorizontal();
    GUILayout.Button(QuickItems[2].name, GUILayout.Height(50));
    GUILayout.Button(QuickItems[3].name, GUILayout.Height(50));
    GUILayout.EndHorizontal();

    GUILayout.EndArea();
}
```

To start off, we access GUILayout and use BeginArea. This is a useful tool to have a contained area to work with. The next step is to activate the BeginHorizontal function within GUILayout, which ensures that everything we put on the GUI is in an even, horizontal line. After this, we create GUILayout buttons, one for each slot in our inventory. We set the text of the button to the amount and name of an item within the inventory, then we set the height of the button.

We do this a few times to show all of our inventory items on screen in three different rows. After this, we do the same thing for `QuickItems`, except with two rows of two items. Now, the player can see their inventory by clicking on one of our custom inputs.

Playtesting

Now that we've created our inventory and can show it on the GUI, let's set up a test scene and try out our new inventory.

Creating a test scene

To start off, create a new scene and name it `"Chapter 4"`. After this, create two empty GameObjects, name one of them `"Inventory"` and the other one `"Empty"`. Drag `Empty` to `Inventory`, creating a parent-child relationship. This is what your hierarchy should look like now:

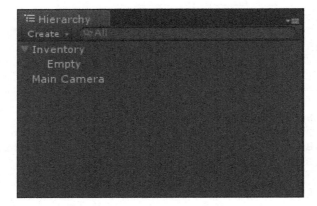

Once you've done this, drag the `Inventory` script to the `Inventory` GameObject. Set the **X** position of **Inventory Rect** to `300` and its **Y** position to `200`. Then in **Inv Items**, set the **Size** value to `9` and in **Quick Items** set its **Size** value to `4`. After this, drag the `Empty` GameObject to the empty slot next to **Empty Object** in the **Inspector** panel. This is what the **Inspector** panel of the `Inventory` GameObject should look like now:

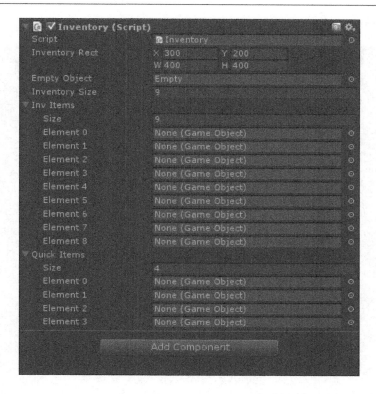

Once you have done this, the scene is ready to be tested. Now run the scene and press the *I* key; the inventory GUI should pop up on the screen. The GUI should look like what is shown in the following screenshot:

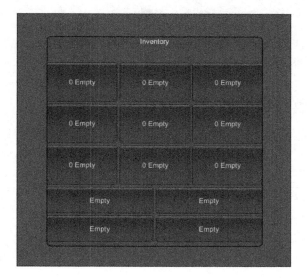

Also, the inspector should look like this:

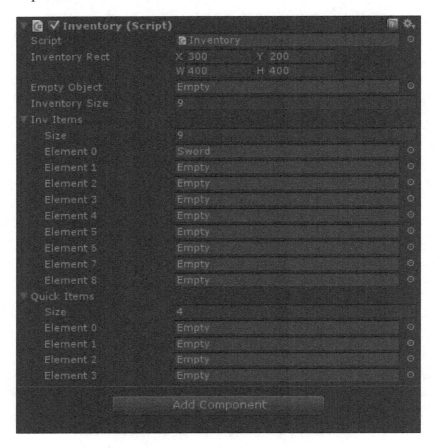

Our inventory works without any errors! Now let's see whether we can add and remove items just as easily.

Let's add an item

To test whether we can add items to our inventory, we're going to add a bit of code to the Update function:

```
if(Input.GetButtonUp("Fire1"))
{
  GameObject test = new GameObject();
  test.name = "Sword";

  AddToInventory(4, test);
}
```

When we click on the left mouse button, we create a new GameObject. We set the new GameObject's name to `"Sword"`. Then we call the `AddToInventory` function, passing 4 and `test`. Here, 4 is the amount that we want to add to the item count and `test` is the new GameObject that we want to add. Now, run the scene and press *I*. Once the GUI is visible, click on the left mouse button a few times. Your screen should look something like this:

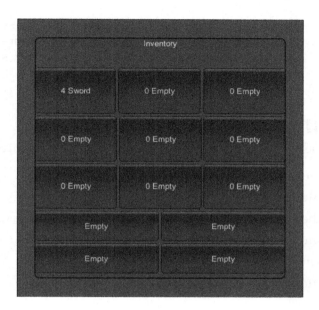

As you can see, the new item is placed in our inventory. The name of the object as well as its amount is shown. Now, you'll notice that in the **Inspector** panel you have a lot of empty GameObjects added to the scene. This is because you created multiple new GameObjects within your test code. Your **Inspector** panel should look like what is shown in the previous screenshot as well.

Let's remove some items

We can now add items to the inventory, so let's see whether we can remove them too. Add this bit of code under our previous test code:

```
if(Input.GetButtonUp("Fire2"))
{
  GameObject test2 = new GameObject();
  test2.name = "Sword";

  RemoveFromInventory(2, test2);
}
```

When we click the right mouse button, we again create a new GameObject. We also set its name to "Sword" and then call the RemoveFromInventory function. In the function call, we pass the 2 and the test2 GameObject. Now, when we run our game and click the right mouse button, it will remove two of the sword objects from our inventory. If "Sword" has a value of zero or less, the inventory slot will be set to our Empty object.

To make sure this works, run the scene and left click your mouse a few times to add a bunch of swords to the inventory. Now right-click a few times to remove some swords. You can even remove them until you don't have any swords left and the slot will be empty.

Other things to try out

Here's a list of other ways you can try to test the inventory even further:

- Make the inventory size larger or smaller
- Remove multiple different items from the inventory
- Remove the empty spaces from the GUI display of the inventory
- Add a button that organizes the inventory by amount and/or by alphabet
- Make the inventory GUI window moveable by the player
- Add a button that resets the inventory to make it empty

Summary

In this chapter, you learned one way of creating an inventory system. You may find other ways to create an inventory, but this method should suffice to add an inventory to any game that you create. With this inventory, you can add items, remove items, have multiples of items, set some quick-items, and finally show the inventory as a GUI display.

In the next chapter, we will create Artificial Intelligence, more commonly known as AI. We'll create a simple behavior system to call different events that the AI can do. The AI will run what we'll call internal events, essentially doing stuff that affects the AI GameObject itself. Next we'll create external events, which are actions that will cause the AI to affect other GameObjects such as attacking or moving around the game world. Finally, we'll create an AI manager and learn how to play character animations.

5
Enemy and Friendly AIs

Artificial Intelligence, also known as **AI**, is something that you'll see in every video game that you play. First-person shooter, real-time strategy, simulation, role playing games, sports, puzzles, and so on, all have various forms of AI in both large and small systems. In this chapter, we'll be going over several topics that involve creating AI, including techniques, actions, pathfinding, animations, and the AI manager. Then, finally, we'll put it all together to create an AI package of our own.

In this chapter, you will learn:

- What a finite state machine is
- What a behavior tree is
- How to combine two AI techniques for complex AI
- How to deal with internal and external actions
- How to handle outside actions that affect the AI
- How to play character animations
- What is pathfinding?
- How to use a waypoint system
- How to use Unity's NavMesh pathfinding system
- How to combine waypoints and NavMesh for complete pathfinding

AI techniques

There are two very common techniques used to create AI: the finite state machine and the behavior tree. Depending on the game that you are making and the complexity of the AI that you want, the technique you use will vary. In this chapter, we'll utilize both the techniques in our AI script to maximize the potential of our AI.

Finite state machines

Finite state machines are one of the most common AI systems used throughout computer programming. To define the term itself, a finite state machine breaks down to a system, which controls an object that has a limited number of states to exist in. Some real-world examples of a finite state machine are traffic lights, television, and a computer. Let's look at an example of a computer finite state machine to get a better understanding.

A computer can be in various states. To keep it simple, we will list three main states. These states are On, Off, and Active. The Off state is when the computer does not have power running it, the On state is when the computer does have power running it, and the Active state is when someone is using the computer. Let's take a further look into our computer finite state machine and explore the functions of each of its states:

State	Functions
On	• Can be used by anyone • Can turn off the computer
Off	• Can turn on the computer • Computer parts can be operated on
Active	• Can access the Internet and various programs • Can communicate with other devices • Can turn off the computer

Each state has its own functions. Some of the functions of each state affect each other, while some do not. The functions that do affect each other are the functions that control what state the finite state machine is in. If you press the power button on your computer, it will turn on and change the state of your computer to On. While the state of your computer is On, you can use the Internet and possibly some other programs, or communicate to other devices such as a router or printer. Doing so will change the state of your computer to Active. When you are using the computer, you can also turn off the computer by its software or by pressing the power button, therefore changing the state to Off.

In video games, you can use a finite state machine to create AI with a simple logic. You can also combine finite state machines with other types of AI systems to create a unique and perhaps more complex AI system. In this chapter, we will be using finite state machines as well as what is known as a **behavior tree**.

The behavior tree form of the AI system

A behavior tree is another kind of AI system that works in a very similar way to finite state machines. Actually, behavior trees are made up of finite state machines that work in a hierarchical system. This system of hierarchy gives us great control over an individual, and perhaps many finite state systems within the behavior tree, allowing us to have a complex AI system.

Taking a look back at the table explaining a finite state machine, a behavior tree works the same way. Instead of states, you have behaviors, and in place of the state functions, you have various finite state machines that determine what is done while the AI is in a specific behavior. Let's take a look at the behavior tree that we will be using in this chapter to create our AI:

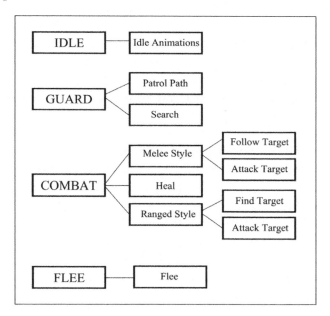

On the left-hand side, we have four behaviors: **Idle**, **Guard**, **Combat**, and **Flee**. To the right are the finite state machines that make up each of the behaviors. **Idle** and **Flee** only have one finite state machine, while **Guard** and **Combat** have multiple. Within the **Combat** behavior, two of its finite state machines even have a couple of their own finite state machines.

As you can see, this hierarchy-based system of finite state machines allows us to use a basic form of logic to create an even more complex AI system. At the same time, we are also getting a lot of control by separating our AI into various behaviors. Each behavior will run its own silo of code, oblivious to the other behaviors. The only time we want a behavior to notice another behavior is either when an internal or external action occurs that forces the behavior of our AI to change.

Combining the techniques

In this chapter, we will take both of the AI techniques and combine them to create a great AI package. Our behavior tree will utilize finite state machines to run the individual behaviors, creating a unique and complex AI system. This AI package can be used for an enemy AI as well as a friendly AI.

Let's start scripting!

Now, let's begin scripting our AI! To start off, create a new C# file and name it `AI_Agent`. Upon opening it, delete any functions within the main class, leaving it empty. Just after the `using` statements, add this enum to the script:

```
public enum Behaviors {Idle, Guard, Combat, Flee};
```

This enum will be used throughout our script to determine what behavior our AI is in. Now let's add it to our class. It is time to declare our first variable:

```
public Behaviors aiBehaviors = Behaviors.Idle;
```

This variable, `aiBehaviors`, will be the deciding factor of what our AI does. Its main purpose is to have its value checked and changed when needed. Let's create our first function, which will utilize one of this variable's purposes:

```
void RunBehaviors()
{
  switch(aiBehaviors)
  {
  case Behaviors.Idle:
    RunIdleNode();
    break;
  case Behaviors.Guard:
    RunGuardNode();
    break;
  case Behaviors.Combat:
    RunCombatNode();
    break;
  case Behaviors.Flee:
```

```
        RunFleeNode();
        break;
    }
}
```

What this function will do is check the value of our `aiBehaviors` variable in a switch statement. Depending on what the value is, it will then call a function to be used within that behavior. This function is actually going to be a finite state machine, which will decide what that behavior does at that point. Now, let's add another function to our script, which will allow us to change the behavior of our AI:

```
void ChangeBehavior(Behaviors newBehavior)
{
    aiBehaviors = newBehavior;

    RunBehaviors();

}
```

As you can see, this function works very similarly to the `RunBehaviors` function. When this function is called, it will take a new `behaviors` variable and assign its value to `aiBehaviors`. By doing this, we changed the behavior of our AI. Now let's add the final step to running our behaviors; for now, they will be empty functions that act as placeholders for our internal and external actions. Add these functions to the script:

```
void RunIdleNode()
{

}

void RunGuardNode()
{

}

void RunCombatNode()
{

}

void RunFleeNode()
{

}
```

Each of these functions will run the finite state machines that make up the behaviors. These functions are essentially a *middleman* between the behavior and the behavior's action. Using these functions is the beginning of having more control over our behaviors, something that can't be done with a simple finite state machine.

Internal and external actions

The actions of a finite state machine can be broken up into internal and external actions. Separating the actions into the two categories makes it easier to define what our AI does in any given situation. The separation is helpful in the planning phase of creating AI, but it can also help in the scripting part as well, since you will know what will and will not be called by other classes and GameObjects. Another way this separation is beneficial is that it eases the work of multiple programmers working on the same AI; each programmer could work on separate parts of the AI without as many conflicts.

External actions

External actions are functions and activities that are activated when objects outside of the AI object act upon the AI object. Some examples of external actions include being hit by a player, having a spell being cast upon the player, falling from heights, losing the game by an external condition, communicating with external objects, and so on.

The external actions that we will be using for our AI are:

- Changing its health
- Raising a stat
- Lowering a stat
- Killing the AI

Internal actions

Internal actions are the functions and activities that the AI runs within itself. Examples of these are patrolling a set path, attacking a player, running away from the player, using items, and so on. These are all actions that the AI will choose to do depending on a number of conditions.

The internal actions that we will be using for our AI are:

- Patrolling a path
- Attacking a player
- Fleeing from a player
- Searching for a player

Scripting the actions

It's time to add some internal and external actions to the script. First, be sure to add the `using` statement to the top of your script with the other `using` statements:

```
using System.Collections.Generic;
```

Now, let's add some variables that will allow us to use the actions:

```
public bool isSuspicious = false;
public bool isInRange = false;
public bool FightsRanged = false;
public List<KeyValuePair<string, int>> Stats = new
List<KeyValuePair<string, int>>();
public GameObject Projectile;
```

The first three of our new variables are conditions to be used in finite state machines to determine what function should be called. Next, we have a list of the `KeyValuePair` variables, which will hold the stats of our AI GameObject. The last variable is a GameObject, which is what we will use as a projectile for ranged attacks.

Remember the empty middleman functions that we previously created? Now with these new variables, we will be adding some code to each of them. Add this code so that the empty functions are now filled:

```
void RunIdleNode()
{
  Idle();
}

void RunGuardNode()
{
  Guard();
}

void RunCombatNode()
{
  if(FightsRanged)
```

```
      RangedAttack();
   else
      MeleeAttack();
}

void RunFleeNode()
{
   Flee();
}
```

Two of the three boolean variables we just created are being used as conditionals to call different functions, effectively creating finite state machines. Next, we will be adding the rest of our actions; these are what is being called by the middleman functions. Some of these functions will be empty placeholders, but will be filled later on in the chapter:

```
void Idle()
{
}

void Guard()
{
   if(isSuspicious)
   {
      SearchForTarget();
   }
   else
   {
      Patrol();
   }
}

void Combat()
{
   if(isInRange)
   {
      if(FightsRanged)
      {
         RangedAttack();
      }
      else
      {
         MeleeAttack();
      }
   }
}
```

```
    else
    {
      SearchForTarget();
    }
}

void Flee()
{
}

void SearchForTarget()
{
}

void Patrol()
{
}

void RangedAttack()
{
  GameObject newProjectile;
  newProjectile = Instantiate(Projectile, transform.position,
Quaternion.identity) as GameObject;
}

void MeleeAttack()
{
}
```

In the Guard function, we check to see whether the AI notices the player or not.
If it does, then it will proceed to search for the player; if not, then it will continue to
patrol along its path. In the Combat function, we first check to see whether the player
is within the attacking range; if not, then the AI searches again. If the player is within
the attacking range, we check to see whether the AI prefers attacking up close or
far away.

For ranged attacks, we first create a new, temporary GameObject variable. Then,
we set it to an instantiated clone of our Projectile GameObject. From here, the
projectile will run its own scripts to determine what it does. This is how we allow
our AI to attack the player from a distance.

To finish off our actions, we have two more functions to add. The first one will be to change the health of the AI, which is as follows:

```
void ChangeHealth(int Amount)
{
  if(Amount < 0)
  {
    if(!isSuspicious)
    {
      isSuspicious = true;
      ChangeBehavior(Behaviors.Guard);
    }
  }
  for(int i = 0; i < Stats.Capacity; i++)
  {
    if(Stats[i].Key == "Health")
    {
      int tempValue = Stats[i].Value;
      Stats[i] = new KeyValuePair<string, int>(Stats[i].Key, tempValue
+= Amount);
      if(Stats[i].Value <= 0)
      {
        Destroy(gameObject);
      }
      else if(Stats[i].Value < 25)
      {
        isSuspicious = false;
        ChangeBehavior(Behaviors.Flee);
      }
      break;
    }
  }
}
```

This function takes an `int` variable, which is the amount by which we want to change the health of the player. The first thing we do is check to see if the amount is negative; if it is, then we make our AI suspicious and change the behavior accordingly. Next, we search for the health stat in our list and set its value to a new value that is affected by the `Amount` variable. We then check if the AI's health is below zero to kill it; if not, then we also check if its health is below 25. If the health is that low, we make our AI flee from the player.

To finish off our actions, we have one last function to add. It will allow us to affect a specific stat of the AI. These modifications will either add to or subtract from a stat. The modifications can be permanent or restored anytime. For the following instance, the modifications will be permanent:

```
void ModifyStat(string Stat, int Amount)
{
  for(int i = 0; i < Stats.Capacity; i++)
  {
    if(Stats[i].Key == Stat)
    {
      int tempValue = Stats[i].Value;
      Stats[i] = new KeyValuePair<string, int>(Stats[i].Key, tempValue
+= Amount);
      break;
    }
  }
  if(Amount < 0)
  {
    if(!isSuspicious)
    {
      isSuspicious = true;
      ChangeBehavior(Behaviors.Guard);
    }
  }
}
```

This function takes a string and an integer. The string is used to search for the specific stat that we want to affect and the integer is how much we want to affect that stat by. It works in a very similar way to how the ChangeHealth function works, except that we first search for a specific stat. We also check to see if the amount is negative. This time, if it is negative, we change our AI behavior to Guard. This seems to be an appropriate response for the AI after being hit by something that negated one of its stats!

Pathfinding

Pathfinding is how the AI will maneuver around the level. For our AI package, we will be using two different kinds of pathfinding, NavMesh and waypoints. The waypoint system is a common approach to create paths for AI to move around the game level. To allow our AI to move through our level in an intelligent manner, we will use Unity's NavMesh component.

Creating paths using the waypoint system

Using waypoints to create paths is a common practice in game design, and it's simple too. To sum it up, you place objects or set locations around the game world; these are your waypoints. In the code, you will place all of your waypoints that you created in a container of some kind, such as a list or an array. Then, starting at the first waypoint, you tell the AI to move to the next waypoint. Once that waypoint has been reached, you send the AI off to another one, ultimately creating a system that iterates through all of the waypoints, allowing the AI to move around the game world through the set paths. Although using the waypoint system will grant our AI movement in the world, at this point, it doesn't know how to avoid obstacles that it may come across. That is when you need to implement some sort of mesh navigation system so that the AI won't get stuck anywhere.

Unity's NavMesh system

The next step in creating AI pathfinding is to create a way for our AI to navigate through the game world intelligently, meaning that it does not get stuck anywhere. In just about every game out there that has a 3D-based AI, the world it inhabits has all sorts of obstacles. These obstacles could be plants, stairs, ramps, boxes, holes, and so on. To get our AI to avoid these obstacles, we will use Unity's NavMesh system, which is built into Unity itself.

Setting up the environment

Before we can start creating our pathfinding system, we need to create a level for our AI to move around in. To do this, I am just using Unity primitive models such as cubes and capsules. For the floor, create a cube, stretch it out, and squish it to make a rectangle. From there, clone it several times so that you have a large floor made up of cubes.

Next, delete a bunch of the cubes and move some others around. This will create holes in our floor, which will be used and tested when we implement the NavMesh system. To make the floor easy to see, I've created a material in green and assigned it to the floor cubes.

After this, create a few more cubes, make one really long and one shorter than the previous one but thicker, and the last one will be used as a ramp. I've created an intersection of the really long cube and the thick cube. Then, place the ramp towards the end of the thick cube, giving access to the top of the cubes.

Our final step in creating our test environment is to add a few waypoints for our AI. For testing purposes, create five waypoints in this manner. Place one in each corner of the level and one in the middle. For the actual waypoints, use the capsule primitive. For each waypoint, add a rigid body component. Name the waypoints as Waypoint1, Waypoint2, Waypoint3, and so on. The name is not all that important for our code; it just makes it easier to distinguish between waypoints in the inspector. Here's what I made for my level:

Creating the NavMesh

Now, we will create the navigation mesh for our scene. The first thing we will do is select all of the floor cubes. In the menu tab in Unity, click on the **Window** option, and then click on the **Navigation** option at the bottom of the dropdown; this will open up the **Navigation** window. This is what you should be seeing right now:

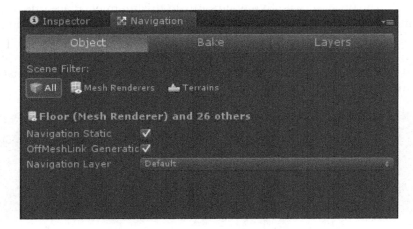

By default, the **OffMeshLink Generation** option is not checked; be sure to check it. What this does is create links at the edges of the mesh allowing it to communicate with any other **OffMeshLink** nearby, creating a singular mesh. This is a handy tool since game levels typically use more than one mesh as a floor.

The **Scene** filter will just show specific objects within the hierarchy view list. Selecting all the objects will show all of your GameObjects. Selecting mesh renderers will only show GameObjects that have the mesh renderer component. Then, finally, if you select terrains, only terrains will be shown in the **Hierarchy** view list.

The **Navigation Layer** dropdown will allow you to set the area as either **walkable**, **not walkable**, or **jump accessible**. Walkable areas typically refer to floors, ramps, and so on. Non-walkable areas refer to walls, rocks, and other various obstacles.

Next, click on the **Bake** tab next to the **Object** tab. You should see information that looks like this:

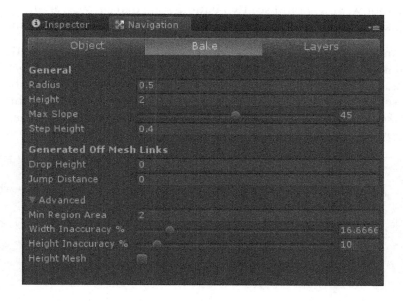

For this chapter, I am leaving all the values at their defaults. The **Radius** property is used to determine how close to the walls the navigation mesh will exist. **Height** determines how much vertical space is needed for the AI agent to be able to walk on the navigation mesh. **Max Slope** is the maximum angle that the AI is allowed to travel on for ramps, hills, and so on. The **Step Height** property is used to determine how high the AI can step up onto surfaces higher than the ground level.

For **Generated Off Mesh Links**, the properties are very similar to each other. The **Drop Height** value is the maximum amount of space the AI can intelligently drop down to another part of the navigation mesh. **Jump Distance** is the opposite of **Height**; it determines how high the AI can jump up to another part of the navigation mesh.

The **Advanced** options are to be used when you have a better understanding of the NavMesh component and want a little more out of it. Here, you can further tweak the accuracy of the NavMesh as well as create **Height Mesh** to coincide with the navigation mesh.

Now that you know all the basics of the Unity NavMesh, let's go ahead and create our navigation mesh. At the bottom-right corner of the **Navigation** tab in the **Inspector** window, you should see two buttons: one that says **Clear** and the other that says **Bake**. Click on the **Bake** button now to create your new navigation mesh.

Select the ramp and the thick cube that we created earlier. In the **Navigation** window, make sure that the **OffMeshLink Generation** option is not checked, and that **Navigation Layer** is set to **Default**. If the ramp and the thick cube are not selected, reselect the floor cubes so that you have the floors, ramp, and thick wall selected. Bake the navigation mesh again to create a new one. This is what my scene looks like now with the navigation mesh:

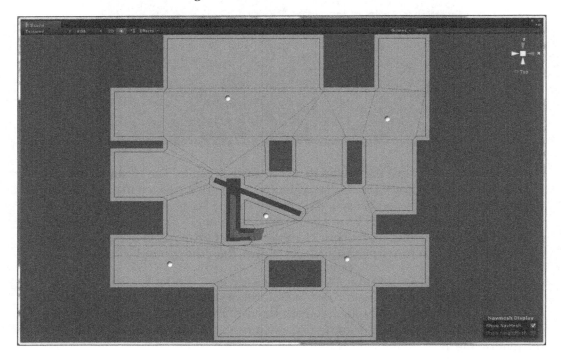

You should be able to see the newly generated navigation mesh overlaying the underlying mesh. This is what was created using the default **Bake** properties. Changing the **Bake** properties will give you different results, which will come down to what kind of navigation mesh you want the AI to use. Now that we have a navigation mesh, let's create the code for our AI to utilize. First, we will code the waypoint system, and then we will code what is needed for the NavMesh system.

Adding our variables

To start our navigation system, we will need to add a few variables first. Place these with the rest of our variables:

```
public Transform[] Waypoints;
public int curWaypoint = 0;
bool ReversePath = false;
NavMeshAgent navAgent;
Vector3 Destination;
float Distance;
```

The first variable is an array of `Transforms`; this is what we will use to hold our waypoints. Next, we have an integer that is used to iterate through our `Transform` array. We have a `bool` variable, which will decide how we should navigate through the waypoints.

The next three variables are more oriented towards our navigation mesh that we created earlier. The `NavMeshAgent` object is what we will reference when we want to interact with the navigation mesh. The destination will be the location that we want the AI to move towards. The distance is what we will use to check how far away we are from that location.

Scripting the navigation functions

Previously, we created many empty functions; some of these are dependent on pathfinding. Let's start with the `Flee` function. Add this code to replace the empty function:

```
void Flee()
{
  for(int fleePoint = 0; fleePoint < Waypoints.Length; fleePoint++)
  {
    Distance = Vector3.Distance(gameObject.transform.position,
Waypoints[fleePoint].position);
    if(Distance > 10.00f)
    {
      Destination = Waypoints[curWaypoint].position;
      navAgent.SetDestination(Destination);
      break;
    }
    else if(Distance < 2.00f)
    {
      ChangeBehavior(Behaviors.Idle);
    }
  }
}
```

What this `for` loop does is pick a waypoint that has `Distance` of more than 10. If it does, then we set the `Destination` value to the current waypoint and move the AI accordingly. If the distance from the current waypoint is less than 2, we change the behavior to `Idle`.

The next function that we will adjust is the `SearchForTarget` function. Add the following code to it, replacing its previous emptiness:

```
void SearchForTarget()
{
  Destination = GameObject.FindGameObjectWithTag("Player").transform.
position;
  navAgent.SetDestination(Destination);
  Distance = Vector3.Distance(gameObject.transform.position,
Destination);
  if(Distance < 10)
    ChangeBehavior(Behaviors.Combat);
}
```

This function will now be able to search for a target, the `Player` target to be more specific. We set `Destination` to the player's current position, and then move the AI towards the player. When `Distance` is less than 10, we set the AI behavior to `Combat`.

Now that our AI can run from the player as well as chase them down, let's utilize the waypoints and create paths for the AI. Add this code to the empty `Patrol` function:

```
void Patrol()
{
  Distance = Vector3.Distance(gameObject.transform.position,
Waypoints[curWaypoint].position);
  if(Distance > 2.00f)
  {
    Destination = Waypoints[curWaypoint].position;
    navAgent.SetDestination(Destination);
  }
  else
  {
    if(ReversePath)
    {
      if(curWaypoint <= 0)
      {
        ReversePath = false;
      }
```

```
        else
        {
          curWaypoint--;
          Destination = Waypoints[curWaypoint].position;
        }
      }
      else
      {
        if(curWaypoint >= Waypoints.Length - 1)
        {
          ReversePath = true;
        }
        else
        {
          curWaypoint++;
          Destination = Waypoints[curWaypoint].position;
        }
      }
    }
  }
```

What `Patrol` will now do is check the `Distance` variable. If it is far from the current waypoint, we set that waypoint as the new destination of our AI. If the current waypoint is close to the AI, we check the `ReversePath` Boolean variable. When `ReversePath` is `true`, we tell the AI to go to the previous waypoint, going through the path in the reverse order. When `ReversePath` is `false`, the AI will go on to the next waypoint in the list of waypoints.

With all of this completed, you now have an AI with pathfinding abilities. The AI can also patrol a path set by waypoints and reverse the path when the end has been reached. We have also added abilities for the AI to search for the player as well as flee from the player.

Character animations

Animations are what bring the characters to life visually in the game. From basic animations to super realistic movements, all the animations are important and really represent what scripters do to the player. Before we add animations to our AI, we first need to get a model mesh for it!

Importing the model mesh

For this chapter, I am using a model mesh that I got from the Unity Asset Store. To use the same model mesh that I am using, go to the Unity Asset Store and search for *Skeletons Pack*. It is a package of four skeleton model meshes that are fully textured, propped, and animated. The asset itself is free and great to use.

When you import the package into Unity, it will come with all four models as well as their textures, and an example scene named ShowCase. Open that scene and you should see the four skeletons. If you run the scene, you will see all the skeletons playing their idle animations.

Choose the skeleton you want to use for your AI; I chose **skeletonDark** for mine. Click on the drop-down list of your skeleton in the **Hierarchy** window, and then on the **Bip01** drop-down list. Then, select the **magicParticle** object. For our AI, we will not need it, so delete it from the **Hierarchy** window.

Create a new prefab in the **Project** window and name it Skeleton. Now select the skeleton that you want to use from the **Hierarchy** window and drag it onto the newly created prefab. This will now be the model that you will use for this chapter.

In your AI test scene, drag and drop **Skeleton Prefab** onto the scene. I have placed mine towards the center of the level, near the waypoint in the middle. In the **Inspector** window, you will be able to see the **Animation** component full of animations for the model.

Now, we will need to add a few components to our skeleton. Go to the **Components** menu on the top of the **Unity** window, select **Navigation**, and then select **NavMesh Agent**. Doing this will allow the skeleton to utilize the NavMesh we created earlier. Next, go into the **Components** menu again and click on **Capsule Collider** as well as **Rigidbody**. Your **Inspector** window should now look like this after adding the components:

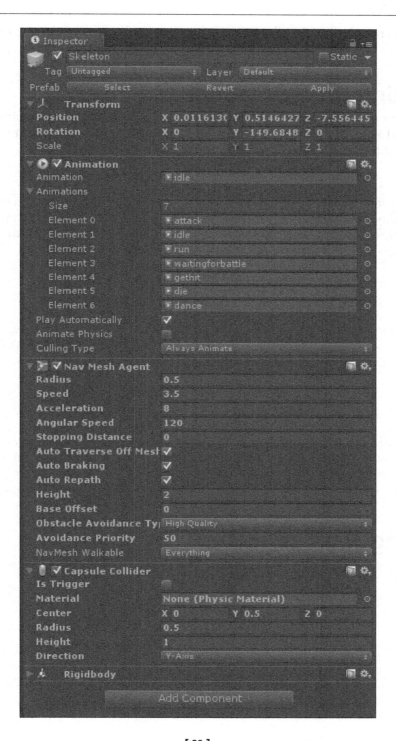

Your model now has all the necessary components needed to work with our AI script.

Scripting the animations

To script our animations, we will take a simple approach to it. There won't be a lot of code to deal with, but we will spread it out in various areas of our script where we need to play the animations. In the `Idle` function, add this line of code:

```
animation.Play("idle");
```

This simple line of code will play the `idle` animation. We use animation to access the model's animation component, and then use the `Play` function of that component to play the animation. The `Play` function can take the name of the animation to call the correct animation to be played; for this one, we call the `idle` animation.

In the `SearchForTarget` function, add this line of code to the script:

```
animation.Play("run");
```

We access the same function of the animation component and call the `run` animation to play here. Add the same line of code to the `Patrol` function as well, since we will want to use that animation for that function too.

In the `RangedAttack` and `MeleeAttack` functions, add this code:

```
animation.Play("attack");
```

Here, we call the `attack` animation. If we had a separate animation for ranged attacks, we would use that instead, but since we don't, we will utilize the same animation for both attack types. With this, we finished coding the animations into our AI. It will now play those animations when they are called during gameplay.

Putting it all together

To wrap up our AI package, we will now finish up the script and add it to the skeleton.

Final coding touches

At the beginning of our AI script, we created some variables that we have yet to properly assign. We will do that in the Start function. We will also add the Update function to run our AI code. Add these functions to the bottom of the class:

```
void Start()
{
   navAgent = GetComponent<NavMeshAgent>();

   Stats.Add(new KeyValuePair<string, int>("Health", 100));
   Stats.Add(new KeyValuePair<string, int>("Speed", 10));
   Stats.Add(new KeyValuePair<string, int>("Damage", 25));
   Stats.Add(new KeyValuePair<string, int>("Agility", 25));
   Stats.Add(new KeyValuePair<string, int>("Accuracy", 60));
}

void Update ()
{
   RunBehaviors();
}
```

In the Start function, we first assign the navAgent variable by getting the NavMeshAgent component from the GameObject. Next, we add new KeyValuePair variables to the Stats array. The Stats array is now filled with a few stats that we created.

The Update function calls the RunBehaviors function. This is what will keep the AI running; it will run the correct behavior as long as the AI is active.

Filling out the inspector

To complete the AI package, we will need to add the script to the skeleton, so drag the script onto the skeleton in the **Hierarchy** window. In the **Size** property of the waypoints array, type the number 5 and open up the drop-down list. Starting with Element 0, drag each of the waypoints into the empty slots.

For the projectile, create a sphere GameObject and make it a prefab. Now, drag it onto the empty slot next to **Projectile**. Finally, set the AI **Behaviors** to **Guard**. This will make it so that when you start the scene, your AI will be patrolling. The **Inspector** window of the skeleton should look something like this:

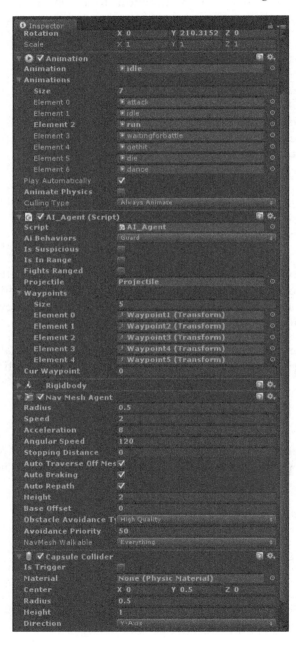

Your AI is now ready for gameplay! To make sure everything works, we will need to do some playtesting.

Playtesting

A great way to playtest the AI is to play the scene in every behavior. Start off with **Guard**, then run it in **Idle**, **Combat**, and **Flee**. For different outputs, try adjusting some of the variables in the **NavMesh Agent** component, such as **Speed**, **Angular Speed**, and **Stopping Distance**. Try mixing your waypoints around so the path is different.

Summary

In this chapter, you learned how to create an AI package. We explored a couple of techniques to handle AI, such as finite state machines and behavior trees. Then, we dived into AI actions, both internal and external. From there, we figured out how to implement pathfinding with both a waypoint system and Unity's NavMesh system. Finally, we topped the AI package off with animations and put everything together, creating our finalized AI.

In the next chapter, you will learn how to create a stat tracking system. To do this, we will add stats and attributes to the player and enemies. Then, we will track stats for both the player and enemies. We will also add an achievement system for some of the stats.

6
Keeping Score

In many games, having stats and scores are a way of showing the players how far along they've come. For some games, stats decide whether players win or lose the game or rounds they play. There are some games where stats create competition such as a high score table in a racing game, or a ranking system in a first-person shooter game. Stats can be used in many ways. They can influence a player to do things they normally wouldn't do, just to get that stat.

In this chapter, we will:

- Create stats for the player
- Implement those stats in our scripts
- Create a stat tracker for the stats
- Create an achievement system
- Use `PlayerPrefs` to save our stats
- Use GUI methods to show the stats and achievements
- Create/assign the stats

Before we implement our stats, we need to figure out what stats we want to keep track of. This is a rudimentary yet an important step.

Prototype stats

Now let's figure out which stats we want to keep track of! In this book, the game we create will have a gladiator arena-styled gameplay. So we will have rounds where the player will fight enemies. To win a round, the player will need to kill all of the enemies; to lose a round, the enemies will have to kill the player.

Here's a list of stats that we want to track:

- Kills
- Deaths
- Total gold
- Current gold
- Gold spent
- Level
- Rounds won
- Rounds lost
- Kill-death ratio
- Win-lose ratio
- Time played

Assigning the stats to the player

Now that we know what stats we want to track in our game, let's start our script. Create a new C# script and name it StatTracker. Next, let's add our variables to it; these will be the stats that we track:

```
int pKills = 0;
int pDeaths = 0;
int pTotalGold = 0;
int pCurrentGold = 0;
int pGoldSpent = 0;
int pLevel = 1;
int pRoundsWon = 0;
int pRoundsLost = 0;
float pKDR = 0.00f;
float pWLR = 0.00f;
float pTimePlayed = 0.00f;
```

As you can see, the variable names are preceded by the letter p, which, in this instance, will mean that these variables are for the player. Most of our stats are being tracked as int variables; the last few are float. These are the variables that we will modify, save, and reset in our script.

The stat tracker

Our next step is to give our stat tracker all the functionalities that we need. Here, we will create methods to set and reset stats, set and reset `PlayerPrefs`, and save `PlayerPrefs`. Finally, we create a way to show our stats on the screen. `Playerprefs` are functions built in Unity that allow storage of strings, integers, and floats using a system similar to `Dictionary` or `KeyValuePair`.

Setting the stats

The first function that we will create will allow us to set values to specific stats. Add this function to your script:

```
void SetStat(string stat, int intValue = 0)
{
  switch(stat)
  {
  case "Kills":
    pKills+= intValue;

    float fKills = pKills;
    float fDeaths = pDeaths;
      if(fKills != 0)
      pKDR = fDeaths / fKills;
    break;
  case "Deaths":
    pDeaths+= intValue;

    float fKills2 = pKills;
    float fDeaths2 = pDeaths;
      if(fKills2 != 0)
      pKDR = fDeaths2 / fKills2;
    break;
  case "TotalGold":
    pTotalGold+= intValue;
    break;
  case "CurrentGold":
    pCurrentGold+= intValue;
    break;
  case "GoldSpent":
    pGoldSpent+= intValue;
    break;
```

```
case "Level":
  pLevel+= intValue;
  break;
case "RoundsWon":
  pRoundsWon+= intValue;

  float fWins = pRoundsWon;
  float fLosses = pRoundsLost;
  if(fWins != 0)
    pWLR = fLosses / fWins;
  break;
case "RoundsLost":
  pRoundsLost+= intValue;

  float fWins2 = pRoundsWon;
  float fLosses2 = pRoundsLost;
  if(fWins2 != 0)
    pWLR = fLosses2 / fWins2;
  break;
case "TimePlayed":
  pTimePlayed+= fltValue;
  break;
  }
}
```

What this function does is to first take two parameters, the stat we want to modify and an integer value. The integer is set to 0 by default; this is to help avoid possible errors. Next, we run a `switch` statement based on the `stat` string that we passed to decide which of our stats we want to modify.

Kills, deaths, rounds won, and rounds lost have some unique properties. When we set them, we add the new value to the stat, and then we calculate a ratio. When we set kills and deaths, we also do a bit of math to assign the kill-death ratio stat. For rounds won and lost, we also set the rounds won-lost ratio.

Resetting the stats

To reset our stats, we will add a basic but important function to our script, shown as follows:

```
void ResetStats()
{
  pKills = 0;
  pDeaths = 0;
```

```
    pTotalGold = 0;
    pCurrentGold = 0;
    pGoldSpent = 0;
    pLevel = 1;
    pRoundsWon = 0;
    pRoundsLost = 0;
    pKDR = 0.00f;
    pWLR = 0.00f;
    pTimePlayed = 0.00f;
}
```

When this function is called, it will reset all of our stats to their base value. This value is 0 for everything but the player's level, which is 1. If we wanted to reset a specific stat to its base value, we can call the previous function that we created, which is SetStat.

Resetting all of our prefs

To save our stats, we will use Unity's PlayerPrefs. These are a handy way to save small bits of data. They can be used across several platforms and are easy to use. Our first function that we'll create will let us reset our PlayerPrefs value. Add this function to the script:

```
void ResetAllPrefs()
{
    PlayerPrefs.SetInt("PlayerKills", 0);
    PlayerPrefs.SetInt("PlayerDeaths", 0);
    PlayerPrefs.SetInt("PlayerTotalGold", 0);
    PlayerPrefs.SetInt("PlayerCurrentGold", 0);
    PlayerPrefs.SetInt("PlayerGoldSpent", 0);
    PlayerPrefs.SetInt("PlayerLevel", 0);
    PlayerPrefs.SetInt("PlayerRoundsWon", 0);
    PlayerPrefs.SetInt("PlayerRoundsLost", 0);
    PlayerPrefs.SetFloat("PlayerKDR", 0.00f);
    PlayerPrefs.SetFloat("PlayerWLR", 0.00f);
    PlayerPrefs.SetFloat("PlayerTimePlayed", 0.00f);
    PlayerPrefs.Save();
}
```

What this function does is set each PlayerPref value to its base value. When they are all reset, we call a native Save function within PlayerPrefs to save our new values.

Saving all of our prefs

The next function that we will create will allow us to save all of our `PlayerPrefs` values. This will be done in a similar way to how we reset all `PlayerPrefs`. Let's add this new function now:

```
void SaveAllPrefs()
{
  PlayerPrefs.SetInt("PlayerKills", pKills);
  PlayerPrefs.SetInt("PlayerDeaths", pDeaths);
  PlayerPrefs.SetInt("PlayerTotalGold", pTotalGold);
  PlayerPrefs.SetInt("PlayerCurrentGold", pCurrentGold);
  PlayerPrefs.SetInt("PlayerGoldSpent", pGoldSpent);
  PlayerPrefs.SetInt("PlayerLevel", pLevel);
  PlayerPrefs.SetInt("PlayerRoundsWon", pRoundsWon);
  PlayerPrefs.SetInt("PlayerRoundsLost", pRoundsLost);
  PlayerPrefs.SetFloat("PlayerKDR", pKDR);
  PlayerPrefs.SetFloat("PlayerWLR", pWLR);
  PlayerPrefs.SetFloat("PlayerTimePlayed", pTimePlayed);
  PlayerPrefs.Save();
}
```

This function is essentially the same as the `ResetAllPrefs` function, except we change the value at which we assign `PlayerPrefs`. We assign all of the `PlayerPrefs` functions their appropriate stats, and then at the end of the function, we save the `PlayerPrefs` values.

Setting a specific pref

To set a specific pref, we will create a function similar to how we set a specific stat. Add this function to the script:

```
void SetPref(string Pref, int intValue = 0, float fltValue = 0.00f)
{
  if(intValue != 0)
  {
    if(PlayerPrefs.HasKey(Pref))
      PlayerPrefs.SetInt(Pref, intValue);
  }
  if(fltValue != 0.00f)
  {
    if(PlayerPrefs.HasKey(Pref))
      PlayerPrefs.SetFloat(Pref, fltValue);
  }

  PlayerPrefs.Save();
}
```

This function will take the `PlayerPref` function we want to set and also a value that we want to set it to. Inside the function, we will check to see which value is not set to 0. If one of the values are still 0, we ignore that value type. If one of the values is not 0, we check to see whether the `PlayerPref` function passed to the function exists. If that function exists, we then set the `PlayerPref` value accordingly and finish off by saving our `PlayerPrefs` values.

Resetting a specific pref

What if you wanted to reset a specific PlayerPref value? For this, we will create a slightly different function that will allow us to do that. Add this new function to our script:

```
void ResetPref(string Pref)
{
  switch(Pref)
  {
  case "Kills":
    PlayerPrefs.SetInt("PlayerKills", 0);
    break;
  case "Deaths":
    PlayerPrefs.SetInt("PlayerDeaths", 0);
    break;
  case "TotalGold":
    PlayerPrefs.SetInt("PlayerTotalGold", 0);
    break;
  case "CurrentGold":
    PlayerPrefs.SetInt("PlayerCurrentGold", 0);
    break;
  case "GoldSpent":
    PlayerPrefs.SetInt("PlayerGoldSpent", 0);
    break;
  case "Level":
    PlayerPrefs.SetInt("PlayerLevel", 0);
    break;
  case "RoundsWon":
    PlayerPrefs.SetInt("PlayerRoundsWon", 0);
    break;
  case "RoundsLost":
    PlayerPrefs.SetInt("PlayerRoundsLost", 0);
    break;
  case "KDR":
    PlayerPrefs.SetFloat("PlayerKDR", 0.00f);
    break;
  case "WLR":
    PlayerPrefs.SetFloat("PlayerWLR", 0.00f);
    break;
```

```
    case "TimePlayed":
      PlayerPrefs.SetFloat("PlayerTimePlayed", 0.00f);
      break;
  }

  PlayerPrefs.Save();
}
```

For this function, we pass one variable that we want to reset, which is `PlayerPref`. Then, we run a `switch` statement for the string that we passed to decide which `PlayerPref` function to reset. After we reset `PlayerPref`, we save it.

Showing our stats on the screen

Our final step in creating our stats is to show them on the screen. To do this, we will need to first add a couple of more variables:

```
public bool showStats = false;
public Rect statsRect = new Rect(Screen.width / 2, Screen.height / 2,
400, 400);
```

The new `bool` variable will decide whether we can show the stats menu, and the `Rect` variable is the area in which the stats menu will be. Next, we will add the `OnGUI` function that will draw our GUI on the screen:

```
void OnGUI()
{
  if(showStats)
  {
    statsRect = GUI.Window(0, statsRect, StatsGUI, "Stats");
  }
}
```

In the `OnGUI` function, we check the `showStats` Boolean variable to see whether or not the stats menu will be seen on the screen. You can see that it calls a function named `StatsGUI`. This function is what draws everything to the screen; let's add that function now:

```
void StatsGUI(int ID)
{
  GUILayout.BeginArea(new Rect(15, 25, 400, 400));

  GUILayout.BeginVertical();
  GUILayout.Label("Level - " + pLevel);
  GUILayout.Label("Gold - " + pCurrentGold);
```

```
GUILayout.Label("Kills - " + pKills);
GUILayout.Label("Deaths - " + pDeaths);
GUILayout.Label("Kill/Death Ratio - " + pKDR);
GUILayout.Label("Rounds Won - " + pRoundsWon);
GUILayout.Label("Rounds Loss - " + pRoundsLost);
GUILayout.Label("Win/Loss Ratio - " + pWLR);
GUILayout.Label("Time Played (in minutes) - " + (pTimePlayed /
60.00f));
GUILayout.EndVertical();

GUILayout.EndArea();
}
```

To draw our stats on the screen, we use labels to show some text as well as the associating variables. For the `Time Played` stat, we divide it by 60 so it will show how many minutes have passed. In Unity, time is tracked by seconds, so we show minutes instead so that there isn't a large and possibly confusing number shown to the player.

To give our script a quick test, create a new scene and place the script onto the camera. Be sure to set the `showStats` Boolean variable to `true` in the **Inspector** window. You should see this on your screen:

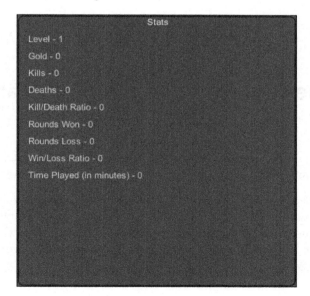

Each of the stats we wanted to track is now shown on the screen in a vertical list. Later in this book, when we put everything together to finish our game, we will tie this into our menu system.

The achievement system

Achievements are being used now in just about every game out there. You can see them across all genres and gaming platforms, achievements are everywhere. They give the player a sense of pride and accomplishment, knowing that they did something so much that they get rewarded for it. Achievements are also a way for players to brag and show off what they've done in their game.

Prototyping the achievements

Similar to how we prototyped our stats, we will need to prototype the achievements. The stats will be used to unlock achievements, but not every stat will have an achievement for it. For this reason, we will have fewer achievements than stats, but we will have different levels for each achievement.

Here's a list of the achievements that we will track:

- Kills
- Total gold
- Gold spent
- Level
- Rounds won
- Time played

Adding the required achievement variables

To get things started, create a new C# script and name it AchievementSystem. Next, let's create our variables:

```
int achKills, achTotGold, achGoldSpnt, achLvl, achRndsW, achTime;
bool getKills, getTotGold, getGoldSpnt, getLvl, getRndsW, getTime;
```

The integer variables are what we will use to track which level the players are on within that achievement. Achievement levels can be used to allow the player to unlock further achievements of a specific stat. The bool variables will be used to determine whether the player can continue to unlock more achievement levels of a specific achievement.

Resetting the achievements

The first function that we will add to our achievement system will allow us to reset our achievements to a base value. Add this next function to the script:

```
void ResetAchievements()
{
  achKills = 0;
  achTotGold = 0;
  achGoldSpnt = 0;
  achLvl = 0;
  achRndsW = 0;
  achTime = 0;
  getKills = true;
  getTotGold = true;
  getGoldSpnt = true;
  getLvl = true;
  getRndsW = true;
  getTime = true;
}
```

Within the preceding function, we set all of our achievement level variables to 0 and the `bool` variables to `true`.

Achievement trackers

In this part of the chapter, we will add trackers for each of our achievements. Each tracker will have its own function. The functions will be very similar to each other, but will have their own variables to affect.

When the functions are called, it'll take in an integer; this integer is the amount of the stat that we want to check. Within the function, we check with our `bool` variables to see whether that achievement can still be gained. Next, we check the amount in order to iterate the achievement level appropriately.

Once the achievement level is at its highest amount, we disable the ability to gain more achievements for that skill.

Tracking the kills

Our first tracker will track the player kills; let's add the tracker function now:

```
void Kills(int Amount)
{
  if(getKills)
  {
    if(Amount >= 10 && Amount < 49)
    {
      if(achKills != 1)
        achKills++;
    }
    if(Amount >= 50 && Amount < 99)
    {
      if(achKills != 2)
        achKills++;
    }
    if(Amount >= 100 && Amount < 249)
    {
      if(achKills != 3)
        achKills++;
    }
    if(Amount >= 250 && Amount < 499)
    {
      if(achKills != 4)
        achKills++;
    }
    if(Amount >= 500 && Amount < 999)
    {
      if(achKills != 5)
        achKills++;
    }
    if(Amount >= 1000)
    {
      if(achKills != 6)
        achKills = 6;
    }
    if(achKills == 6)
      getKills = false;
  }
}
```

Tracking the gold total

The next tracker will track how much gold the player gained in the entire time they played the game. Add this function to the script:

```
void TotalGold(int Amount)
{
  if(getTotGold)
  {
    if(Amount >= 100 && Amount < 249)
    {
      if(achTotGold != 1)
        achTotGold++;
    }
    if(Amount >= 250 && Amount < 499)
    {
      if(achTotGold != 2)
        achTotGold++;
    }
    if(Amount >= 500 && Amount < 999)
    {
      if(achTotGold != 3)
        achTotGold++;
    }
    if(Amount >= 1000 && Amount < 4999)
    {
      if(achTotGold != 4)
        achTotGold++;
    }
    if(Amount >= 5000 && Amount < 9999)
    {
      if(achTotGold != 5)
        achTotGold++;
    }
    if(Amount >= 10000)
    {
      if(achTotGold != 6)
        achTotGold = 6;
    }

    if(achTotGold == 6)
      getTotGold = false;
  }
}
```

Tracking the gold spent

This tracker will track how much gold the player spent on items during the time they played the game:

```
void GoldSpent(int Amount)
{
  if(getGoldSpnt)
  {
    if(Amount >= 100 && Amount < 249)
    {
      if(achGoldSpnt != 1)
        achGoldSpnt++;
    }
    if(Amount >= 250 && Amount < 499)
    {
      if(achGoldSpnt != 2)
        achGoldSpnt++;
    }
    if(Amount >= 500 && Amount < 999)
    {
      if(achGoldSpnt != 3)
        achGoldSpnt++;
    }
    if(Amount >= 1000 && Amount < 4999)
    {
      if(achGoldSpnt != 4)
        achGoldSpnt++;
    }
    if(Amount >= 5000 && Amount < 9999)
    {
      if(achGoldSpnt != 5)
        achGoldSpnt++;
    }
    if(Amount >= 10000)
    {
      if(achGoldSpnt != 6)
        achGoldSpnt = 6;
    }

    if(achGoldSpnt == 6)
      getGoldSpnt = false;
  }
}
```

Tracking the player's level

This will track the player's level in the game. A player can increase their level in any way you wish within the game:

```
void Level(int Amount)
{
  if(getLvl)
  {
    if(Amount >= 5 && Amount < 9)
    {
      if(achLvl != 1)
        achLvl++;
    }
    if(Amount >= 10 && Amount < 24)
    {
      if(achLvl != 2)
        achLvl++;
    }
    if(Amount >= 25 && Amount < 49)
    {
      if(achLvl != 3)
        achLvl++;
    }
    if(Amount >= 50 && Amount < 74)
    {
      if(achLvl != 4)
        achLvl++;
    }
    if(Amount >= 75 && Amount < 99)
    {
      if(achLvl != 5)
        achLvl++;
    }
    if(Amount >= 100)
    {
      if(achLvl != 6)
        achLvl = 6;
    }

    if(achLvl == 6)
      getLvl = false;
  }
}
```

Tracking the rounds won

This will track how many rounds the player has won overall:

```
void RoundsWon(int Amount)
{
  if(getRndsW)
  {
    if(Amount >= 5 && Amount < 9)
    {
      if(achRndsW != 1)
        achRndsW++;
    }
    if(Amount >= 10 && Amount < 24)
    {
      if(achRndsW != 2)
        achRndsW++;
    }
    if(Amount >= 25 && Amount < 49)
    {
      if(achRndsW != 3)
        achRndsW++;
    }
    if(Amount >= 50 && Amount < 74)
    {
      if(achRndsW != 4)
        achRndsW++;
    }
    if(Amount >= 75 && Amount < 99)
    {
      if(achRndsW != 5)
        achRndsW++;
    }
    if(Amount >= 100)
    {
      if(achRndsW != 6)
        achRndsW = 6;
    }

    if(achRndsW == 6)
      getRndsW = false;
  }
}
```

Tracking the time played

This tracker will track how long the player played the game. Unity tracks time in seconds; we will track the time stat in minutes, so we will be dividing the time by 60:

```
void TimePlayed(float Amount)
{
  if(getTime)
  {
    float minutes = Amount / 60.00f;

    if(minutes >= 10.00f && minutes < 59.00f)
    {
      if(achTime != 1)
        achTime++;
    }
    if(minutes >= 60.00f && minutes < 119.00f)
    {
      if(achTime != 2)
        achTime++;
    }
    if(minutes >= 120.00f && minutes < 179.00f)
    {
      if(achTime != 3)
        achTime++;
    }
    if(minutes >= 180.00f && minutes < 239.00f)
    {
      if(achTime != 4)
        achTime++;
    }
    if(minutes >= 240.00f && minutes < 299.00f)
    {
      if(achTime != 5)
        achTime++;
    }
    if(minutes >= 300.00f)
    {
      if(achTime != 6)
        achTime = 6;
    }

    if(achTime == 6)
      getTime = false;
  }
}
```

Let's check the achievements

Next, we will add the functions that will actually check for achievements. These are the functions we will call when we want to check whether the player's stats have unlocked any achievements.

Checking a specific achievement

The CheckAchievement function will allow us to check for a single achievement. It takes a string, which is the achievement to check for. From here, it runs a switch statement to decide which achievement to modify. Add this function to your script. This function can be used when loading a menu, which shows the player's achievements and can be used to prevent unlocking the same achievement more than once:

```
void CheckAchievement(string Achievement)
{
  switch(Achievement)
  {
  case "Kills":
    Kills(PlayerPrefs.GetInt("PlayerKills"));
    break;
  case "TotalGold":
    TotalGold(PlayerPrefs.GetInt("PlayerTotalGold"));
    break;
  case "GoldSpent":
    GoldSpent(PlayerPrefs.GetInt("PlayerGoldSpent"));
    break;
  case "Level":
    Level(PlayerPrefs.GetInt("PlayerLevel"));
    break;
  case "RoundsWon":
    RoundsWon(PlayerPrefs.GetInt("PlayerRoundsWon"));
    break;
  case "TimePlayed":
    TimePlayed(PlayerPrefs.GetFloat("PlayerTimePlayed"));
    break;
  }
}
```

Checking all of the achievements

The CheckAllAchievements function will allow us to check all the achievements.
Let's add the function now:

```
void CheckAllAchievements()
{
  Kills(PlayerPrefs.GetInt("PlayerKills"));
  TotalGold(PlayerPrefs.GetInt("PlayerTotalGold"));
  GoldSpent(PlayerPrefs.GetInt("PlayerGoldSpent"));
  Level(PlayerPrefs.GetInt("PlayerLevel"));
  RoundsWon(PlayerPrefs.GetInt("PlayerRoundsWon"));
  TimePlayed(PlayerPrefs.GetFloat("PlayerTimePlayed"));
```

Displaying the achievements on screen

Just as we did with the stats, we will have a new menu for achievements.
First, we'll start by adding a couple of variables:

```
public bool showAchievements = false;
public Rect achRect = new Rect(Screen.width / 2, Screen.height / 2,
700, 700);
```

Adding the GUI functions

Now, we will add the functions to show the achievements on the screen.
The first function is the OnGUI function, which we will add now:

```
void OnGUI()
{
  if(showAchievements)
  {
    achRect = GUI.Window(0, achRect, AchGUI, "Achievements");
  }
}
```

Just as in the stats menu, we check whether we want to show the achievements
menu. If we do it, is shown on screen; if not, we hide it.

Next, we will add the AchGUI function that is being called in the OnGUI function.
This is a large function, but it will allow us to show the achievements that we need.
It is similar to the stat menu, except we will show buttons instead of a number.
We use buttons just as a proof of concept; normally, you would use an image for
your achievements.

What this function will do is use a switch statement to check the level of each achievement that we track. Then, it will show the number of achievement buttons onscreen according to what level the player is at, within that achievement. Let's add the new function now:

```
void AchGUI(int ID)
{
   GUILayout.BeginArea(new Rect(15, 25, 700, 700));

   GUILayout.BeginVertical();
   GUILayout.Label("Level");
   GUILayout.Label("Kills");
   GUILayout.Label("Total Gold");
   GUILayout.Label("Gold Spent");
   GUILayout.Label("Rounds Won");
   GUILayout.Label("Time Played");
   GUILayout.EndVertical();

   GUILayout.EndArea();

   GUILayout.BeginArea(new Rect(50, 25, 700, 700));

   GUILayout.BeginHorizontal();
   if(achLvl >= 1)
      GUILayout.Button("Level 1", GUILayout.Height(25), GUILayout.
Width(75));
      if(achLvl >= 2)
      GUILayout.Button("Level 2", GUILayout.Height(25), GUILayout.
Width(75));
      if(achLvl >= 3)
      GUILayout.Button("Level 3", GUILayout.Height(25), GUILayout.
Width(75));
      if(achLvl >= 4)
      GUILayout.Button("Level 4", GUILayout.Height(25), GUILayout.
Width(75));
      if(achLvl >=5)
      GUILayout.Button("Level 5", GUILayout.Height(25), GUILayout.
Width(75));
      if(achLvl >=6)
      GUILayout.Button("Level 6", GUILayout.Height(25), GUILayout.
Width(75));
   GUILayout.EndHorizontal();

   GUILayout.BeginHorizontal();
```

```
    if(achKills >= 1)
        GUILayout.Button("Kills 1", GUILayout.Height(25), GUILayout.
Width(75));
    if(achKills >= 2)
        GUILayout.Button("Kills 2", GUILayout.Height(25), GUILayout.
Width(75));
    if(achKills >= 3)
        GUILayout.Button("Kills 3", GUILayout.Height(25), GUILayout.
Width(75));
    if(achKills >= 4)
        GUILayout.Button("Kills 4", GUILayout.Height(25), GUILayout.
Width(75));
    if(achKills >=5)
        GUILayout.Button("Kills 5", GUILayout.Height(25), GUILayout.
Width(75));
    if(achKills >=6)
        GUILayout.Button("Kills 6", GUILayout.Height(25), GUILayout.
Width(75));
  GUILayout.EndHorizontal();
  GUILayout.EndArea();

  GUILayout.BeginArea(new Rect(90, 80, 700, 700));
  GUILayout.BeginHorizontal();
  if(achTotGold >= 1)
        GUILayout.Button("Total Gold 1", GUILayout.Height(25),
GUILayout.Width(75));
    if(achTotGold >= 2)
        GUILayout.Button("Total Gold 2", GUILayout.Height(25),
GUILayout.Width(75));
    if(achTotGold >= 3)
        GUILayout.Button("Total Gold 3", GUILayout.Height(25),
GUILayout.Width(75));
    if(achTotGold >= 4)
        GUILayout.Button("Total Gold 4", GUILayout.Height(25),
GUILayout.Width(75));
    if(achTotGold >=5)
        GUILayout.Button("Total Gold 5", GUILayout.Height(25),
GUILayout.Width(75));
    if(achTotGold >=6)
        GUILayout.Button("Total Gold 6", GUILayout.Height(25),
GUILayout.Width(75));
  GUILayout.EndHorizontal();

  GUILayout.BeginHorizontal();
```

```
    if(achGoldSpnt >= 1)
        GUILayout.Button("Gold Spent 1", GUILayout.Height(25),
GUILayout.Width(75));
    if(achGoldSpnt >= 2)
        GUILayout.Button("Gold Spent 2", GUILayout.Height(25),
GUILayout.Width(75));
    if(achGoldSpnt >= 3)
        GUILayout.Button("Gold Spent 3", GUILayout.Height(25),
GUILayout.Width(75));
    if(achGoldSpnt >= 4)
        GUILayout.Button("Gold Spent 4", GUILayout.Height(25),
GUILayout.Width(75));
    if(achGoldSpnt >=5)
        GUILayout.Button("Gold Spent 5", GUILayout.Height(25),
GUILayout.Width(75));
    if(achGoldSpnt >=6)
        GUILayout.Button("Gold Spent 6", GUILayout.Height(25),
GUILayout.Width(75));
    GUILayout.EndHorizontal();

    GUILayout.BeginHorizontal();
    if(achRndsW >= 1)
        GUILayout.Button("Rounds Won 1", GUILayout.Height(25),
GUILayout.Width(75));
    if(achRndsW >= 2)
        GUILayout.Button("Rounds Won 2", GUILayout.Height(25),
GUILayout.Width(75));
    if(achRndsW >= 3)
        GUILayout.Button("Rounds Won 3", GUILayout.Height(25),
GUILayout.Width(75));
    if(achRndsW >= 4)
        GUILayout.Button("Rounds Won 4", GUILayout.Height(25),
GUILayout.Width(75));
    if(achRndsW >=5)
        GUILayout.Button("Rounds Won 5", GUILayout.Height(25),
GUILayout.Width(75));
    if(achRndsW >=6)
        GUILayout.Button("Rounds Won 6", GUILayout.Height(25),
GUILayout.Width(75));
    GUILayout.EndHorizontal();

    GUILayout.BeginHorizontal();
```

```
    if(achTime >= 1)
        GUILayout.Button("Time Played 1", GUILayout.Height(25),
GUILayout.Width(75));
      if(achTime >= 2)
        GUILayout.Button("Time Played 2", GUILayout.Height(25),
GUILayout.Width(75));
      if(achTime >= 3)
        GUILayout.Button("Time Played 3", GUILayout.Height(25),
GUILayout.Width(75));
      if(achTime >= 4)
        GUILayout.Button("Time Played 4", GUILayout.Height(25),
GUILayout.Width(75));
      if(achTime >=5)
        GUILayout.Button("Time Played 5", GUILayout.Height(25),
GUILayout.Width(75));
      if(achTime >=6)
        GUILayout.Button("Time Played 6", GUILayout.Height(25),
GUILayout.Width(75));
    GUILayout.EndHorizontal();

    GUILayout.EndArea();
}
```

For testing purposes, I made the achievement level variables public and set them to various values. Drag the script onto the camera, remove the stats script, and set the showAchievements Boolean value to true. If you run the scene, you should see the following results:

You will probably have slightly different results, based on what you assigned each of the achievement level variables.

Playtesting

To playtest the stats and achievements GUI, you can change the values that show on screen and make sure the correct values are shown on screen. Other than that, you can call each of the functions individually in a Start function to make sure that they work. To take this chapter a bit further, you can add stats to track as well as show achievements for them. You can also replace the text in the achievements with an image to better represent the achievements; this would be a nice finishing touch to them.

Summary

In this chapter, you learned how to track stats, save them, and show them in a GUI menu. To track the stats, we created interactive functions to modify them. During the creation of the stat saving script, you learned about what PlayerPref function are and how to use them. You also learned how to keep track of achievements and show them on a GUI menu as well.

In the next chapter, you will learn how to add the *save game* functionality to your game. To save the game data, we will create two methods, allowing the player to save the game anytime they want and allowing the game to use checkpoint saving. We will also save using XML files as well as text files.

7
Creating Save and Load Systems

Saving data within a game is very important, which can be seen in just about every game out there. There is all kinds of data that you might want to keep track of, not only for yourself, but also for the player. The player's inventory, enemies' position, the player's statistics, and a lot more can be saved and loaded from a file that you create. In Unity, there are several ways to save data that you can choose from. Earlier in this book, we already went over how to use `PlayerPrefs` to save and load data. In this chapter, you will learn how to use XML and custom flat files, and then create a way to activate your saving and loading processes.

In this chapter, you will:

- Save data to a flat file
- Load data from a flat file
- Customize our flat file
- Save data to an XML file
- Load data from an XML file
- Implement a checkpoint-based system
- Implement an anywhere/anytime saving system

Saving data with flat files

The first and more common way to save data (that we will go over) is using the flat file system. In this style, you can save a normal text file with data from your game and load it later on. We will also discuss how to customize our file so that we can have our own extension added to it. For our flat file system, we will save the player's position as well as our statistics that we created earlier in this book. To start off, we will need to create a new C# script and name it `FLAT_Save_System`.

Adding the required variables

Before we start adding our variables and other code, we need to make sure that we have all the required `using` statements. Add these `using` statements to your code:

```
using UnityEngine;
using System.Collections;
using System.Collections.Generic;
using System;
using System.IO;
using System.Text;
```

For this script, we will only need to create a few public variables; add these to your script:

```
public string sFileName;
public string sDirectory;

public GameObject Player;
```

The first string will be the file that we will save and load from will be called, the name should also include the extension. The next string is the directory that we will save to and load from—for testing purposes and using the `Desktop` directory so that we can easily find it later on. Our final variable, `GameObject`, is our player.

Time to save our file

Now, we will add the function that will allow us to save our flat file. To save our file, we will use the code that we didn't discuss in this book before, as you can see from our new `using` statements. Add this function to your script:

```
void WriteToFile(string file = "")
{
  if(file != "")
```

```
      sFileName = file;

  if(File.Exists(sDirectory + sFileName))
  {
    DeleteFile(sFileName);
  }

  using(StreamWriter sw = new StreamWriter(sDirectory + sFileName))
  {
    sw.WriteLine(PlayerPrefs.GetInt("PlayerKills").ToString());
    sw.WriteLine(PlayerPrefs.GetInt("PlayerDeaths").ToString());
    sw.WriteLine(PlayerPrefs.GetInt("PlayerTotalGold").ToString());
    sw.WriteLine(PlayerPrefs.GetInt("PlayerCurrentGold").ToString());
    sw.WriteLine(PlayerPrefs.GetInt("PlayerGoldSpent").ToString());
    sw.WriteLine(PlayerPrefs.GetInt("PlayerLevel").ToString());
    sw.WriteLine(PlayerPrefs.GetInt("PlayerRoundsWon").ToString());
    sw.WriteLine(PlayerPrefs.GetInt("PlayerRoundsLost").ToString());
    sw.WriteLine(PlayerPrefs.GetFloat("PlayerKDR").ToString());
    sw.WriteLine(PlayerPrefs.GetFloat("PlayerWLR").ToString());
    sw.WriteLine(PlayerPrefs.GetFloat("PlayerTimePlayed").ToString());
    sw.WriteLine(Player.transform.position.x.ToString());
    sw.WriteLine(Player.transform.position.y.ToString());
    sw.WriteLine(Player.transform.position.z.ToString());
  }
}
```

This function takes in a string. We have set the string to a blank value; this will allow us to call the function with or without sending the value. To start off the function, we check whether the file has a value; if it does, then we will use it as our new filename. If it does not, then we will continue to use the filename we previously set in our public variable.

After this, we check whether our file already exists. If it does, we run a function that will delete that file; we will create this function later on in this chapter. We delete the file so that we don't have any issues with duplicate files or incorrect filenames being made.

Next, we start the process of creating and saving our file. To do this, we use a `StreamWriter` type. `StreamWriter` allows us to write data to a file. We use a basic instance of `StreamWriter`, but the class also has other options that can expand upon how you write your data.

To use `StreamWriter`, we set the path that we want to write to, or in this case, the stream, and then add lines to that stream that will be written to our file. To add lines to our file, we call the native `WriteLine` function from the `StreamWriter` class. Within this call, we pass the variable that we want to save. For this instance, we grab `PlayerPrefs` we had set earlier as well as the player's transform position.

Deleting our flat files

Next, we create a function that allows us to delete flat files. Add this function to your script:

```
void DeleteFile(string file = "")
{
  File.Delete(sDirectory + file);
}
```

To delete a file, we use the `Delete` function within the `File` class. Before we delete the file, we make sure that it actually exists using the `Exists` function within the `File` class. The file that we are deleting is the one that is set to our directory and filename variables.

Loading our flat files

For the final feature in our flat file system, we add the loading functionality.

Time to load our file

Now that we have created a way to save information to a flat file, we need to create a way to load that information. To do this, we will use a similar process as the one that we used to save the information. Let's add our final function to the script:

```
void ReadFile(string file = "")
{
  if(file != "")
    sFileName = file;

  using(StreamReader sr = new StreamReader(sDirectory + sFileName))
  {
    int kills = Convert.ToInt32(sr.ReadLine());
    int deaths = Convert.ToInt32(sr.ReadLine());
```

```
        int totgold = Convert.ToInt32(sr.ReadLine());
        int curgold = Convert.ToInt32(sr.ReadLine());
        int level = Convert.ToInt32(sr.ReadLine());
        int rwon = Convert.ToInt32(sr.ReadLine());
        int rlost = Convert.ToInt32(sr.ReadLine());
        float pkdr = Convert.ToSingle(sr.ReadLine());
        float pwlr = Convert.ToSingle(sr.ReadLine());
        float ptime = Convert.ToSingle(sr.ReadLine());
        float x = Convert.ToSingle(sr.ReadLine());
        float y = Convert.ToSingle(sr.ReadLine());
        float z = Convert.ToSingle(sr.ReadLine());
        Player.transform.position = new Vector3(x, y, z);
    }
}
```

To load our data from the file, we will use `StreamReader`. `StreamReader` is very similar to `StreamWriter`, except that it loads data from a file instead of writing to a file. We pass the directory and filename that we want to load into our `StreamReader` class. Next, we read each line using the `ReadLine` function within the `StreamReader` class. For every line that we read, we can assign it to a variable, therefore loading the data.

The XML save system

The next method that we learn under data management is saving and loading from an XML file. Saving and loading from an XML file allows you to get more details on how you save your data. An XML file is made up of tagged lines that allow you to load or save specific data for easier usage. Create a new C# script and name it `XML_Save_System`. Before we write the code to save and load to XML, we need to first create our XML files.

Creating our XML files

To create XML files, we use a program called Notepad++, a free-to-use text editor. Notepad++ is a handy tool to have for situations like these; you can download Notepad++ free of cost from `http://notepad-plus-plus.org/`.

When you open Notepad++, you should first select **Language** at the top of the screen and select **XML**. This will set the current document to use the XML language.

Next, we start adding our tags. First, we make the `PlayerData` XML file. Add these lines so that your XML file looks like mine:

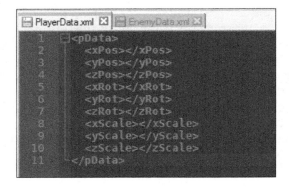

The first tag or node that we create is the `pData` tag, which will be our root node. This will be used to anchor our data and other nodes. The rest of the nodes will be what we save to and load our data from. The actual order of these nodes is irrelevant as long as they're within the root node. Click on the **Save** button, and name this file `PlayerData`. Be sure to click on the **Save as type** option below the filename and select the **XML** option.

Next, we will create the `EnemyData` XML file. Open a new file in Notepad++, and add these lines to your new XML file:

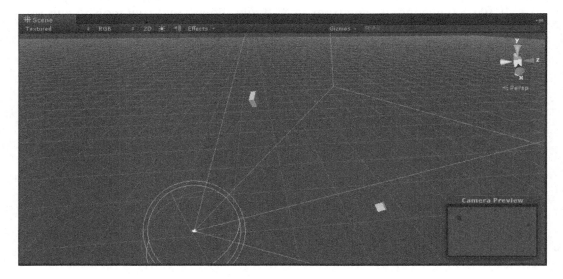

As you can see in the preceding screenshot, this new XML file has a similar structure to that of the `PlayerData` XML file. Our root node is `eData`, and after that, we have an enemy node. The enemy node holds the rest of the nodes that we save to and load from almost like a class or object. You can consider the enemy to be a class and the child nodes within it as the class's properties. The reason we are doing this is to save multiple enemies to our XML file, and they will each have their own data.

Finally, save this file in the same way you did the `PlayerData` XML file, but name this one `EnemyData`. I have placed both of these files to the desktop for testing purposes. Normally, you would keep your saved files in the same directory as your game or in some hidden location.

Saving data with XML

Now, you will learn how to save to your XML files and use the nodes we created within the XML files that we just created.

Adding the required variables

Before we start adding variables, we need to make sure that we have all the `using` statements required. Add these to your script if you don't have them already:

```
using UnityEngine;
using System;
using System.Collections;
using System.Collections.Generic;
using System.Xml;
using System.Xml.Serialization;
using System.IO;
using System.Text;
```

Next, we will add our variables to the script. For an XML-saving system, we will use more variables than we did while using a flat file. This is because, to test our XML system, we will save the player's transform data as well as the transform data for multiple enemies. Add these variables to your script:

```
XmlDocument xPlayer = new XmlDocument();
XmlDocument xEnemy = new XmlDocument();
public string pFileName = "";
public string eFileName = "";
public GameObject Player;
public GameObject[] Enemies;
```

Our first two variables are XML documents; these variables hold the data from our XML files in our computer. The next two strings hold the directory and filename with the extension of the XML files that we are using. Finally, we have two GameObject variables, with the first one being for our player and the other one being an array of GameObjects to hold our enemies.

Saving the player data

Now, we will add the function we will call to save our player data. Add this function to your script:

```
void SavePlayer()
{
  if(Player != null)
  {
    XmlNode root = xPlayer.FirstChild;

    foreach(XmlNode node in root.ChildNodes)
    {
      switch(node.Name)
      {
      case "xPos":
        node.InnerText = Player.transform.position.x.ToString();
        break;
      case "yPos":
        node.InnerText = Player.transform.position.y.ToString();
        break;
      case "zPos":
        node.InnerText = Player.transform.position.z.ToString();
        break;
      case "xRot":
        node.InnerText = Player.transform.rotation.x.ToString();
        break;
      case "yRot":
        node.InnerText = Player.transform.rotation.y.ToString();
        break;
      case "zRot":
        node.InnerText = Player.transform.rotation.z.ToString();
        break;
      case "xScale":
        node.InnerText = Player.transform.localScale.x.ToString();
        break;
      case "yScale":
```

```
        node.InnerText = Player.transform.localScale.y.ToString();
        break;
      case "zScale":
        node.InnerText = Player.transform.localScale.z.ToString();
        break;
      }
    }
    xPlayer.Save(pFileName);
  }
}
```

When we call this function, we first check whether there is actually a GameObject in our `Player` variable. If there isn't, then no saving will be done. Next, we declare an `XmlNode` variable, which will be our root node from the XML document. After this, we run a `foreach` loop that will find all of our child nodes within that root node.

To find specific nodes, we check the name property of that node, which actually is what we typed to create that node. In the switch statement, we look for each node that we want to save data to. For every node in XML, we set its `InnerText` value to its associating value from our player's GameObject. The `InnerText` property of a node is the data it holds and is what we will save to and load from.

Finally, we call the `Save` function from our `xPlayer` `XmlDocument` variable and pass it to the directory and filename we set in our `pFileName` variable.

Saving the enemy data

We will add the function to save our enemy data. This function will look similar to our function to save player data, except with a little more complication since we will be intending this function to save for multiple enemies. Add this function to your script now, just below the `SavePlayer` function:

```
void SaveEnemies()
{
  xEnemy.RemoveAll();

  XmlNode eRoot = xEnemy.CreateNode(XmlNodeType.Element, "eData", "");
  string[] nodes = {"name", "xPos", "yPos", "zPos", "xRot", "yRot",
"zRot", "xScale", "yScale", "zScale"};

  for(int e = 0; e < Enemies.Length; e++)
  {
    if(Enemies[e] != null)
    {
```

```
        XmlNode eBase = xEnemy.CreateNode(XmlNodeType.Element, "enemy",
"");

        for(int n = 0; n < nodes.Length; n++)
        {
            XmlNode newNode = xEnemy.CreateNode(XmlNodeType.Element,
nodes[n], "");

            eBase.AppendChild(newNode);
        }

        foreach(XmlNode node in eBase.ChildNodes)
        {
            switch(node.Name)
            {
            case "name":
                node.InnerText = Enemies[e].name;
                break;
            case "xPos":
                node.InnerText = Enemies[e].transform.position.x.ToString();
                break;
            case "yPos":
                node.InnerText = Enemies[e].transform.position.y.ToString();
                break;
            case "zPos":
                node.InnerText = Enemies[e].transform.position.z.ToString();
                break;
            case "xRot":
                node.InnerText = Enemies[e].transform.rotation.x.ToString();
                break;
            case "yRot":
                node.InnerText = Enemies[e].transform.rotation.y.ToString();
                break;
            case "zRot":
                node.InnerText = Enemies[e].transform.rotation.z.ToString();
                break;
            case "xScale":
                node.InnerText = Enemies[e].transform.
localScale.x.ToString();
                break;
            case "yScale":
                node.InnerText = Enemies[e].transform.
localScale.y.ToString();
                break;
            case "zScale":
                node.InnerText = Enemies[e].transform.
localScale.z.ToString();
                break;
```

```
        }

        eRoot.AppendChild(eBase);
      }
      xEnemy.AppendChild(eRoot);
    }
  }
  xEnemy.Save(eFileName);
}
```

In the first line, we call the RemoveAll function from the xEnemy XmlDocument variable. This deletes all of the nodes from the XML document. We do this for simplicity's sake, this allows us to avoid the hassle of searching for specific enemy nodes to save data from a specific enemy. Next, we create a couple of variables. The first one will be our root node that holds all of our enemies. The next one is a string array, which will hold the names of nodes we will use later on.

The next step in this function is to use a for loop to iterate through our enemies' GameObject array; this is to check whether we actually have an enemy GameObject in our array. If it runs into a null, it won't save any data for that spot.

Once we check to see that we don't have a null GameObject, we start creating our XML data. First, we create a new XmlNode variable, which will be the root node for our enemy data. Next, we run a for loop to create new nodes for each of the variables that we want to save. We do this by creating a new node and setting its name to one of the strings in our nodes string array. Finally, we append it as a child to our enemy root node.

Now that we have created the enemy node and added all of the child nodes that we want to save to, let's iterate through those nodes and start saving our data. To check each node, we create a foreach loop like we did to save the player data and check the names for each of the eBase child nodes.

After finding each of the specific nodes, we assign InnerText with the value associating nodes with the current enemy GameObject. Once all the nodes have been assigned, we append the eBase node to the root node. We do this process for each of the GameObjects within the enemies' GameObject array, saving the data for each of them.

Finally, to end the function, we call the Save function of our xEnemy XML document and save the data to our EnemyData XML document.

Loading data with XML

Our final step in learning how to use XML is to load the data that we just saved to our XML document into our game. While loading the XML data, you will notice that it's a process similar to that of loading from a flat file. The real difference is that instead of loading a line of data, we are loading from a specific part of the saved data.

Loading the player data

To load player data, we will add this function to your script just below the SavePlayer function and above the SaveEnemies function:

```
void LoadPlayer()
{
  float xPos = 0.00f;
  float yPos = 0.00f;
  float zPos = 0.00f;
  float xRot = 0.00f;
  float yRot = 0.00f;
  float zRot = 0.00f;
  float xScale = 0.00f;
  float yScale = 0.00f;
  float zScale = 0.00f;

  if(Player != null)
  {
    XmlNode root = xPlayer.FirstChild;
    foreach(XmlNode node in root.ChildNodes)
    {
      switch(node.Name)
      {
      case "xPos":
        xPos = Convert.ToSingle(node.InnerText);
        break;
      case "yPos":
        yPos = Convert.ToSingle(node.InnerText);
        break;
      case "zPos":
        zPos = Convert.ToSingle(node.InnerText);
        break;
      case "xRot":
```

```
              xRot = Convert.ToSingle(node.InnerText);
              break;
          case "yRot":
              yRot = Convert.ToSingle(node.InnerText);
              break;
          case "zRot":
              zRot = Convert.ToSingle(node.InnerText);
              break;
          case "xScale":
              xScale = Convert.ToSingle(node.InnerText);
              break;
          case "yScale":
              yScale = Convert.ToSingle(node.InnerText);
              break;
          case "zScale":
              zScale = Convert.ToSingle(node.InnerText);
              break;
          }
      }

    Player.transform.position = new Vector3(xPos, yPos, zPos);
    Player.transform.rotation = new Quaternion(xRot, yRot, zRot,
0.00f);
    Player.transform.localScale = new Vector3(xScale, yScale, zScale);
    }
}
```

Before we start loading our data, we need to create some placeholder variables for our data. These will be used later on to load data from the XML document, then be loaded into our player GameObject. Next, we check whether the player GameObject isn't null as a fail-safe, then we start loading our data.

To load our data, we first create an XmlNode root from xPlayer XmlDocument. Then, we run a foreach loop to look for every child node within the root node. We then assign our placeholder variables we just created with the InnerText values from each of the child nodes. Since a string can't be loaded into a float variable, we use the Convert method to make the string into a float for the InnerText values.

Finally, after we load our data from the XML document into our placeholder variables, we start assigning them to our player GameObject. We access the transform of the player and assign the position, rotation, and scale to our new values.

Loading the enemy data

Now, we load our enemy data from our `EnemyData` XML document. This process is similar to loading our player data, except that we will change the code slightly to accommodate multiple GameObjects. Add the following function to your script now just after the `SaveEnemies` function:

```
void LoadEnemies()
{
  string name = "";
  float xPos = 0.00f;
  float yPos = 0.00f;
  float zPos = 0.00f;
  float xRot = 0.00f;
  float yRot = 0.00f;
  float zRot = 0.00f;
  float xScale = 0.00f;
  float yScale = 0.00f;
  float zScale = 0.00f;

  for(int e = 0; e < Enemies.Length; e++)
  {
    if(Enemies[e] != null)
    {
      XmlNode eData = xEnemy.FirstChild;

      XmlNode enemy = eData.ChildNodes[e];

      if(enemy.Name == "enemy")
      {
        foreach(XmlNode eNode in enemy.ChildNodes)
        {
          switch(eNode.Name)
          {
          case "name":
            name = eNode.InnerText;
            break;
          case "xPos":
            xPos = Convert.ToSingle(eNode.InnerText);
            break;
          case "yPos":
            yPos = Convert.ToSingle(eNode.InnerText);
            break;
```

```
    case "zPos":
      zPos = Convert.ToSingle(eNode.InnerText);
      break;
    case "xRot":
      xRot = Convert.ToSingle(eNode.InnerText);
      break;
    case "yRot":
      yRot = Convert.ToSingle(eNode.InnerText);
      break;
    case "zRot":
      zRot = Convert.ToSingle(eNode.InnerText);
      break;
    case "xScale":
      xScale = Convert.ToSingle(eNode.InnerText);
      break;
    case "yScale":
      yScale = Convert.ToSingle(eNode.InnerText);
      break;
    case "zScale":
      zScale = Convert.ToSingle(eNode.InnerText);
      break;
    }

    Enemies[e].name = name;
    Enemies[e].transform.localPosition = new Vector3(xPos, yPos,
zPos);
    Enemies[e].transform.localRotation = new Quaternion(xRot,
yRot, zRot, 0.00f);
    Enemies[e].transform.localScale = new Vector3(xScale,
yScale, zScale);
        }
      }
    }
  }
}
```

Just as we did to load player data, we create placeholder variables. Next, we use a `for` loop to iterate through the enemies' GameObject array and then check to see whether that GameObject is null or not. After this, we go through the process of loading our data.

First, we create the root node and then create the enemy node; these will be the same as those in the `EnemyData` XML. To assign the enemy node, we assign to the current child node within the root node. We match the child node with the enemy GameObject by using the same iterator from the `for` loop.

Next, we check whether the enemy node's name is `enemy` just to verify that we are using the correct node. Then, we use a `foreach` loop to go through each node within the child nodes of the enemy node. Next, we assign the placeholder variables to the associating data from the nodes.

To finish loading our data, we assign each of the placeholder variables to our current GameObject in the enemies' array. Our code will load the correct data for each of the enemies and the data from the XML because we use the iterator from the first `for` loop to choose the correct data from each of the arrays.

Creating the SaveHandler script

Now, we create a script that allows us to call the functions that we just created from the preceding two scripts. First, we create a checkpoint system that saves game data at specific points within the game. Then, we create a way to allow the player to save their data whenever they want to. To get started, create a new script, and name it `SaveHandler`.

The checkpoint system

The first way in which we create to save and load data is a checkpoint system. Checkpoints are typically areas in the game world on reaching which the game will save the player's data. Add this function to allow the checkpoint to save:

```
void OnTriggerEnter(Collider other)
{
  if(other.tag == "SavePoint")
  {
    Camera.main.SendMessage("WriteToFile");
    Destroy(other.gameObject);
  }
}
```

This is a trigger-based method to save. When the player enters the triggered area, the game will save the player's data. Within the `if` statement, you can call any of the save functions we created. You should take note that this function also destroys the trigger object so that the player can't reactivate the checkpoint.

The save anywhere-anytime system

To allow the player to save their data anywhere they want and anytime they want, we add some kind of option for them to call it freely. This can be done by adding to the menu a key or a button, or both, that the player presses. For this example, we will let the player press keys on the keyboard to save and load. Add the following function to create this functionality;

```
void Update()
{
  if(Input.GetKeyUp(KeyCode.F1))
  {
    Camera.main.SendMessage("SaveEnemies");
  }
  if(Input.GetKeyUp(KeyCode.F2))
  {
    Camera.main.SendMessage("LoadEnemies");
  }
}
```

When the player presses the *F1* key, we call the `SaveEnemies` function from the XML save system. If the player presses the *F2* key, we call the `LoadEnemies` function from the XML save system. With this functionality, the players can save their progress at any time.

Playtesting

First let's create a test scene; create a new scene and name it `Saving and Loading Example`. Within this scene, you have Main Camera, which we will use as our player. We need two more GameObjects for our enemies. For the enemies, I created two boxes and placed them randomly in the scene. I've named one of them `Enemy1` and the other `Enemy2`. Here's what my scene looks like:

Where you place the camera and enemy boxes doesn't matter. As long as you have multiple objects to be your enemies, your test scene will be fine. Next, we will add the scripts to Main Camera. First, we will add the `Flat_Save_System` script.

In the **SFile Name** field, type in the name of the file that you want to write to. I've named mine `PlayerData.txt`. In the **SDirectory** field, type the directory you want to save the file to for the desktop type in `C:\Users\USERNAME\Desktop\`. Type your username on your computer in place of username. Finally, drag Main Camera into the slot next to **Player**. Your inspector for that script should look something like the following screenshot.

Now, we will add the `XML_Save_System` script to the camera; go ahead and drag it over to get started. In the **PFileName** field, type in `C:\Users\USERNAME\Desktop\PlayerData.xml`. Do the same for the **EFileName** field, except that you replace `PlayerData.xml` with `EnemyData.xml`. Drag main camera in the slot next to **Player**. In the **Enemies** dropdown, type in the number of enemies you have in your scene. Finally, drag your enemy GameObjects into your `Enemies` array. This is what my **Inspector** menu looks like:

```xml
PlayerData.xml    EnemyData.xml
1   <eData>
2       <enemy>
3           <name>Enemy1</name>
4           <xPos>-26.99181</xPos>
5           <yPos>14.45644</yPos>
6           <zPos>-5.234875</zPos>
7           <xRot>-0.1239236</xRot>
8           <yRot>0.1123635</yRot>
9           <zRot>-0.2062678</zRot>
10          <xScale>2.977825</xScale>
11          <yScale>2.329665</yScale>
12          <zScale>1.241162</zScale>
13      </enemy>
14      <enemy>
15          <name>Enemy2</name>
16          <xPos>6.062684</xPos>
17          <yPos>8.749376</yPos>
18          <zPos>10.63391</zPos>
19          <xRot>0.3671247</xRot>
20          <yRot>-0.2456453</yRot>
21          <zRot>-0.2802415</zRot>
22          <xScale>1</xScale>
23          <yScale>1</yScale>
24          <zScale>1</zScale>
25      </enemy>
26  </eData>
```

Finally, drag the `SaveHandler` script to Main Camera. We will now start testing. Click on the **Play** button at the top, and once the scene has started, press the *F1* key. Doing this will save the enemies' transform. Now click on the scene window, and move your enemy GameObject to a different location, rotate them, and change their size. Once you are done, press the *F2* key. You will notice that the enemy GameObjects will return to their original transform.

Your XML file looks something like the next screenshot. Your XML file might have different values and possibly more enemies.

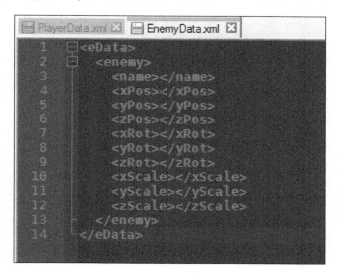

To test the flat file save system, open the `SaveHandler` script to change a couple of values. In the `Update` function, where we check for input, instead of calling `SaveEnemies` and `LoadEnemies`, call `WriteToFile` and `ReadFile`. When you test the scene, again press *F1* to save. On your desktop, you will see a new file called `PlayerData`; open it and you should see several lines with numbers. These numbers are the variables you saved from the game.

If you want to customize your flat file save type and not allow players to easily see or edit the data, change the extension. Instead of saving it as `.txt`, save it as `.save` or anything you want. If the player tries to open it, the computer won't know how to open the file, but the game will still be able to use it.

Summary

In this chapter, you learned how to implement two save systems. You first learned how to save to and load from a flat file. Next, you learned how to save to and load from an XML document. We also went over how to use Notepad++ to create the XML file.

In the next chapter, you will learn how to implement sound into the game. We will go over the background music, atmospheric sounds and sound effects. We will also make the music and atmospheric sounds in both random and playlist styles.

8
Aural Integration

In this chapter, you will learn about adding audio in our game in various ways. Combining the usage of background music, atmospheric sounds, and event-driven sound effects, you will have a game that feels very much alive. Audio plays a major role in how players perceive the game world, and can be as important as graphics in setting the mood of a scene.

In this chapter, you will learn about the following things:

- How to create a random music system
- How to create a playlist-styled music system
- How to integrate and manage atmospheric sounds
- How to create an event-driven sound effects system

Background music

The first part of audio that we will cover will be the background music. Having music in your background can set the mood of a scene, keep the player entertained on a subconscious level, or even be gameplay mechanics that the player interacts with. We will create a dynamic system that will allow us to play songs randomly or in a playlist style.

Creating a random system

The first step in creating our background music system will be to create a new C# script and name it BG_Music_Manager. Before we start scripting, add the using statement to the top of the script using the other using statements:

```
Using System.Collections.Generic;
```

We will need the using statement so that we can use lists. Next, we will create a few variables and add these to our script:

```
public List<AudioClip> SongList = new List<AudioClip>();
public float bgVolume = 1.00f;
public int curSong = 0;
public int ranMin, ranMax;
public bool playRandomly = false;
```

Our first variable is a list of audio clips, which we will use to hold the songs that we want to play in our game. The next variable is float, which will determine how loud our music is. The int variable after that will be used as an iterator for the playlist system when we implement it. The next two integers will be used for our random music system. Finally, the last variable we have is a Boolean value that we will set to pick the system we want for our background music. Now, we will add the function that will play a random song from our list:

```
void PlayRandom()
{
  if(!audio.isPlaying)
  {
    audio.clip = SongList[Random.Range(ranMin, ranMax)];
    audio.Play();
  }
}
```

Before we play a song, we check to see if there is a song playing currently. If there is no song playing, we select a song and play it. To select a song, we grab one from our AudioClip list randomly. To get the random number, we use the minimum and maximum variables we created earlier and place them inside the Range function of the Random class. Using this function will get us a random number between our variables. Once we have a song assigned, we play it.

Adding a playlist system

Next, we will add our function that will run the playlist:

```
void Playlist()
{
  if(!audio.isPlaying)
  {
    if(curSong > SongList.Capacity)
    {
      curSong = 0;
```

```
    }
    else
    {
       curSong++;
    }
    audio.clip = SongList[curSong];
    audio.Play();
  }
}
```

The first thing that we check for when running this function is if there is already a song playing. If there is a song playing, the code will wait until the song stops; if there is no song playing, our code gets executed. To execute the code, we use the iterator variable that we created earlier; if the value is higher than the number of songs we have, we reset it to zero.

If the value of the iterator variable is less than the number of songs we have, then we iterate it and move on to selecting our song. To select the next song to be played, we grab it from the `AudioClip` list and assign it to the `clip` property of the GameObject's `AudioSource` component. Lastly, we call the `Play` function of `AudioSource` to play the song.

Implementing the audio systems

Now that we have created our two systems to play music, we will need to finish off our script with a few other features. First, we will create the `Start` and `Update` functions as they will be needed for this script to work:

```
void Start()
{
  audio.volume = bgVolume;
  ranMax = SongList.Count;
}

void Update()
{
  if(playRandomly)
    PlayRandom();
  else
    Playlist();
}
```

In the Start function, we assign the volume of AudioSource to our volume variable. Next, we set the maximum value to the variable for our random function to the amount of songs that we have in our list. In the Update function, we call the functions that actually play the music. To do this, we check the bool variable that we created earlier to decide which system to use.

An added feature we can place in our script will allow us to play a single song repeatedly. Add this function to the script:

```
void PlayRepeat(AudioClip Song)
{
  audio.clip = Song;
  audio.loop = true;
  audio.Play();
}
```

This function will take the AudioClip value, which will be the song to be played. Next, we assign the song to AudioSource, set its looping property to true, and finally, play it.

The last feature that we will add to our script will allow us to change the speed of the song by using the pitch property. Add this function to the script:

```
void ChangeSpeed(float Speed)
{
  if(Speed > 3)
    Speed = 3;

  if(Speed < -3)
    Speed = -3;

  audio.pitch = Speed;
}
```

This function takes a float variable, which will be used to determine the speed of the song. The maximum speed value is 3, the minimum value is -3, and the default value is 1. When the speed is changed with this function, we check to make sure that the new value is within these boundaries. Once we check the value and it is correct, we set the pitch of AudioSource to the new speed.

Atmospheric sounds

Now, we will create a system to handle atmospheric sounds. Atmospheric sounds are sound effects played in a game to give your scene more immersion. Some good examples are wind blowing in a field, the sounds of drowned out chatter in a pub, your character breathing hard after running for a while, and so on.

Creating the script and variables

To start off, we will need to create a new script and name it `ATM_Manager`. Next, we will create a few variables needed to play our sounds:

```
public List<AudioClip> tmpList = new List<AudioClip>();
public List<string> keys = new List<string>();
public List<KeyValuePair<string, AudioClip>> atmList = new
List<KeyValuePair<string, AudioClip>>();
public float atmVolume = 1.00f;
```

The first three variables that we create are lists. The first of our lists is an `AudioClip` list, which will hold the sound files that we will use. Next, we create a string list, which we will fill with the name of the sound file that we want to call within our code. The last list is a `KeyValuePair` list, which will put together the strings and `AudioClip` variables we just created, and put them in a list that we will call within our code. The last variable we create will be for the volume of the sounds.

Initializing the variables

To give a value to our list that we will use within the code, we will create a `Start` function that initializes the list. Add this to your `Start` function:

```
void Start()
{
  audio.volume = atmVolume;
  int i = 0;
  atmList.Capacity = keys.Capacity;
  foreach(AudioClip ac in tmpList)
  {
    atmList.Add(new KeyValuePair<string, AudioClip>(keys[i], ac));
    i++;
  }
}
```

First, we assign the volume of `AudioSource` to our volume variable. Next, we create an iterator for what we will do next. To assign our internal list, we set its capacity equal to the capacity of the string list. Next, we run a `foreach` loop to check for every `AudioClip` within the temporary list that we created earlier. Finally, for each of the audio clips, we add a new `KeyValuPair` item, which includes the name that we want to call within the code, and the associating `AudioClip` to it.

Playing the atmospheric sounds

We will create two possible ways to play our atmospheric sounds. First, we will allow the sound to play and have it loop, which would be helpful for a rain sound effect or wind sound effect. Add this function to your script:

```
void PlayRepeat(string atmSong)
{
  for(int i = 0; i < atmList.Count; i++)
  {
    if(atmList[i].Key == atmSong)
    {
      audio.clip = atmList[i].Value;
      break;
    }
  }

  audio.loop = true;
  audio.Play();
}
```

This function takes a string. This string will be used to select the sound to be played. A good example for this would be if you wanted to play a rain atmospheric sound, you would have a key that is assigned as `Rain` in your `KeyValuePair` list and its `AudioClip` value would be a rain sound file.

Within the `PlayRepeat` function, we use a `for` loop to iterate through the `KeyValuePair` list. If one of the keys in the `KeyValuePair` list matches the string passed to the `PlayRepeat` function, we assign the clip of the `AudioSource` to that key's value, which would be an `AudioClip`. Lastly, we break the `for` loop, set the `AudioSource` loop property to `true`, and play the sound.

Next, we will add a function that will allow us to play a sound that doesn't loop. Add this function to the script:

```
void Play(string atmSong)
{
  for(int i = 0; i < atmList.Count; i++)
```

```
  {
    if(atmList[i].Key == atmSong)
    {
      audio.clip = atmList[i].Value;
      break;
    }
  }

  audio.loop = false;
  audio.Play();
}
```

This function will run in the same way as the `PlayRepeat` function, except we aren't setting the loop property of the `AudioSource` list. Since the loop property isn't being set to `true`, the sound will only play once.

Sound effects

To play sound effects within our game, we will make an event-based system so that playing the sound effects will be very easy. Sound effects are what bring your items, events, and characters to life! They give your gun the loud bang you would expect, the grunt from your character as they climb a wall, and the notification sound that you get when you hover over an option in the menu. Sound effects add to the immersion of your game and playing them can be very easy.

Creating the script and variables

Our first step in playing sound effects will be to create the C# script and name it `SFX_Manager`. Next, we will need a few variables; add these to your script:

```
public float sfxVolume = 1.00f;
public AudioClip Run, Spell, Strike;
public GameObject RunSource;
```

The first variable should look familiar by now. We will use it for the volume. Next, we create a few audio clips. For this chapter, we will use three specific sound effects for testing purposes. The last variable is a GameObject that will be used to play the running sound effect. Next, let's assign the volume of our sound effects; add this to your `Start` function:

```
public void Start()
{
  audio.volume = sfxVolume;
}
```

Now that we have the volume established, let's add the functions to play our sounds:

```
public void Run()
{
  if(!RunSource.audio.isPlaying)
  {
    RunSource.audio.clip = Run;
    RunSource.audio.Play();
  }
}

public void Spell()
{
  audio.clip = Spell;
  audio.Play();
}

public void Strike()
{
  audio.clip = Strike;
  audio.Play();
}
```

These functions will be the ones you will call to play a sound effect. To play the run sound effect as a looping sound, we check to make sure that the sound has played out before we play it again. This gives the illusion of a looping sound effect. To play the rest of the sounds, we just assign the clip property and play it.

Playtesting

For playtesting, you will need to get a few assets from the Unity Asset Store for the sound effects, background music, and atmospheric sounds. These are the ones I recommend that you use for this example:

- **Future Weapons Set**:
  https://www.assetstore.unity3d.com/en/#!/content/15644

- **Footsteps Sounds Carpet Pack**:
  https://www.assetstore.unity3d.com/en/#!/content/2924

- **The Fantasy Music Collection (Starter)**:
  https://www.assetstore.unity3d.com/en/#!/content/15901

- **The Combat Collection Starter Edition**:
  https://www.assetstore.unity3d.com/en/#!/content/7208

- **Ambient Sample Pack**:
  https://www.assetstore.unity3d.com/en/#!/content/3765

First, create an empty GameObject, name it `RunningSource`, and add an audio source to it; this can be done by navigating to **Add Component | Audio | AudioSource**. On the main camera, add `AudioSource` if there is none. Next, add the `SFX_Manager` script to the camera. For its values, set the following:

- **SFX** volume to 1
- **Run** to `footsteps_runcarpet_1`
- **Spell** to `shot_hand_gun`
- **Strike** to `whoosh_power_fist`
- **Run Source** to the `RunningSource` GameObject

Now open the `SFX_Manager` script and add the `Update` function:

```
public void Update()
{
  if(Input.GetKey(KeyCode.W))
    pRun();

  if(Input.GetButtonUp("Fire1"))
    pStrike();

  if(Input.GetButtonUp("Fire2"))
    pSpell();
}
```

When you test the scene, you can click on the left mouse button to play the strike sound effect. Clicking on the right mouse button will play the spell sound effect. Then, finally, pressing the *W* key will play the running sound effect.

To playtest the atmospheric sounds, a new empty GameObject will need to be created; name it `AtmSource` and be sure to add `AudioSource` and the `ATM_Manager` script to it as well. Set the values of the script to the following:

- **Tmp List** size to 1
- **Element 0** of **Tmp List** to `RainLoop1 - 29 Seconds`
- **Keys** size to 1
- **Keys Element 0** to `Rain`
- **Atm Volume** to 0.75

Lastly, add this line of code to the end of the Start function in the ATM_Manager script:

```
PlayRepeat(atmListt[0].Key);
```

Now, when you test the scene, you will hear the rain sound effect playing as expected. The final part to test is the background music, which will be similar to the way we tested the atmospheric sounds. First, create a new empty GameObject, name it BGMusicSource, and add AudioSource and BG_Music_Manager to it. We will set most of the script's values to their default values except these two:

- **Song List** size to 1
- **Song List Element 0** to maintheme_1_the_combat_collection

Now, in the BG_Music_Manager script, add this line of code at the end of the Start function:

```
PlayRepeat(SongList[0]);
```

When you test the scene now, you should hear everything that we added so far. The background music and the atmospheric sound effect will play, and if you click on the left mouse button or press the *W* key, your sound effects will play as well.

Summary

In this chapter, you learned how to play background music, sound effects, and atmospheric sounds. To play background music we created two unique systems, a random based system and a playlist styled system. Our atmospheric sounds are easy to play as we used a key-based system to call and play sounds with ease. We made a simple yet effective event-based system to play sound effects.

In the next chapter, we will go over the optimization of our game. We will cover how to adjust the graphics, sound, lighting, and many more options to make our games effective and smooth across all platforms.

9
Game Settings

In this chapter, we will be going over optimizations for our game. To optimize our game, we'll add an **Options** menu that will create, save, and load configurations for video and sound. By default, there are some settings given to us by Unity to allow the player to choose what settings they want, but we will allow them to customize their experience.

In this chapter, we'll cover the following topics:

- Creating video configurations
- Creating audio configurations
- Saving and loading custom settings
- Modifying Unity's native settings
- Creating an Options GUI
- Using PlayerPrefs to save settings

Figuring out what to optimize

In almost every video game, there is an **Options** menu with various aspects of the game that you can modify. PC games tend to have the most customizations, but console and handheld games can have many customizations as well. These customizations are made possible by the developer to allow the player to edit how the game outputs to their device and to improve the performance. The most common practice is to make a few preset options available to the player to choose from with varying quality of output. If a player doesn't have a high performance computer, they may need to play the game on low settings, while a player with a great computer can play on the highest settings. Another option is to allow the player to modify different parts of the game output such as shadows or anti-aliasing.

Unity has its own quality settings with various effects on the game. We will be using and editing these settings as well as allowing custom configuration.

Making video configurations

One of the first aspects of the game that we will be editing is the video configuration. When it comes to performance, the video settings are perhaps the most important. Changing something as simple as the shadows can greatly change how a player can smoothly play the game. So let's get started by creating a new C# script and naming it Video_Config.

Setting the values

Our first step in creating video configurations is to create a function that will set a default value for the video settings. For this, we will set the video settings to moderate values that aren't too low or too high. This will give the player a good idea of what they need to modify if they need or want to modify anything:

```
public void SetDefaults()
{
  SetSettings("Medium");
  ToggleShadows(1);
  SetFOV(90.00f);
  SetResolution(0, 1);
  SetAA(2);
  SetVsync(1);
}
```

What this function does is call all of the functions that we create, which will configure the video settings. The values that we send to each of the functions are default settings that aren't too high or too low.

Toggling the shadows

The first video settings that will be affected are the shadows and how they render. In Unity, there are three shadow settings: *None*, *Hard*, and *Soft*. For our game, we'll just use the *None* and *Hard* settings. When we set the shadows to *None*, the shadows will no longer be rendered. When the shadows are set to *Hard*, the shadows will have a hard edge to them; they won't have a fading edge. In the next screenshot, you will see the results of the effects that we used in our game. The image on the left shows the *Hard* shadows and the image on the right shows the shadows turned off.

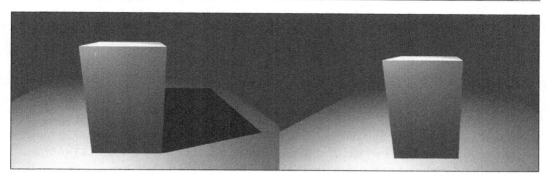

Now that you've seen the resulting effects of our shadow options, let's code these options. Add this function to your script:

```
public void ToggleShadows(int newToggle)
{
   Light[] lights = GameObject.FindObjectsOfType<Light>();

   foreach(Light light in lights)
   {
     if(newToggle == 0)
       light.shadows = LightShadows.None;
     else
       light.shadows = LightShadows.Hard;
   }
}
```

This function takes an `int` value, which will be used to toggle the shadows on or off. Inside the function, we first grab all of the lights within the scene and assign them to an array. Then, for each of the lights, we toggle their shadow's value to *None* or *Hard*. This is how we turn the shadows on or off.

Setting the field of view

The field of view is a video setting that doesn't really affect performance that much, but it is an option that many PC gamers like to modify. The field of view literally means what it's called; it determines how big the view port is for the player to see the game. It's measured by angle degrees and can also be measured vertically, horizontally, or diagonally. Typically, the field of view is measured diagonally for video games.

Add this function to your script:

```
public void SetFOV(float newFOV)
{
   Camera.main.fieldOfView = newFOV;
}
```

The way that cameras in Unity measure the field of view is by using a float variable. So in the preceding function, we receive a float, which will be the new field of view. To change the field of view, we find the main camera, access it's `fieldofView` property, and assign it to the new field of the `view` variable.

Setting the resolution

Next, we'll allow the player to modify the resolution of the game as well as decide whether the game will be full screen or windowed. Add this function to your script:

```
public void SetResolution(int Res, int Full)
{
   bool fs = Convert.ToBoolean(Full);

   switch(Res)
   {
   case 0:
     Screen.SetResolution(1920, 1080, fs);
     break;
   case 1:
     Screen.SetResolution(1600, 900, fs);
     break;
   case 2:
     Screen.SetResolution(1280, 1024, fs);
     break;
   case 3:
     Screen.SetResolution(1280, 800, fs);
     break;
   case 4:
     Screen.SetResolution(640, 400, fs);
     break;
   }
}
```

For this function, we receive two values. The first `int` value decides which resolution we will use and the next `int` value determines whether the game will be full screen or not. Inside the function, we create a `bool` variable, which will be used to determine the fullscreen option. To use the `int` value we passed to the function, we convert the `int` value to a Boolean by using the `Convert` function.

Next, we use a `switch` statement to decide which resolution to set the game to. Which resolutions you want your game to support is up to you, but you should try to support various resolutions because everyone has their own preferences. To set the resolution, we access the `SetResolution` function on the screen, set the resolution values, and then set the `fullscreen` value.

Toggling the anti-aliasing property

The next video setting that we'll modify is the anti-aliasing property. Aliasing in a game is where the models being rendered have jagged edges. Anti-aliasing is what the game renderer does to smooth out those jagged edges. To do this, the renderer will blur the edges slightly to make them smooth. This is one of the options that will make your game look great, but will also slow down the performance. Add this function to your script:

```
public void SetAA(int Samples)
{
   if(Samples == 0 || Samples == 2 || Samples == 4 || Samples == 8)
      QualitySettings.antiAliasing = Samples;
}
```

The way anti-aliasing works is that it will blur the edges by a number of samples. If the number of samples is zero, no anti-aliasing will happen. So for this function, we access the `antiAliasing` property of `QualitySettings` and set it to the `int` value that we pass to the function.

Setting vsync

Vsync affects how the frames are rendered. With vsync *on*, the game will wait until the frame has finished rendering before starting the next frame. With vsync *off*, the game will start to render the next frame while the current frame is still being rendered. The bonus of vsync being off is that the game will render faster but could cause an effect called screen tear, which shows an obvious line on the screen caused by the frames overlapping each other. Add this function to your script:

```
public void SetVsync(int Sync)
{
   QualitySettings.vSyncCount = Sync;
}
```

This function is very similar to the anti-aliasing function. We access the `vSyncCount` property of `QualitySettings` and set it to the `int` value that we pass.

Changing the quality settings

The final video configuration that we'll edit will simply affect the native Unity quality settings. This will be used to quickly change the overall quality settings of the game. Add this function to the script:

```
public void SetSettings(string Name)
{
  switch(Name)
  {
  case "Low":
    QualitySettings.SetQualityLevel(0);
    break;
  case "Medium":
    QualitySettings.SetQualityLevel(1);
    break;
  case "High":
    QualitySettings.SetQualityLevel(2);
    break;
  }
}
```

For this function, we run a `switch` statement on the string that we passed to determine the quality setting. To set the quality setting, we access the `SetQualityLevel` function of `QualitySettings` and set it to the associating quality level.

Loading the settings

The final function that we will add will allow us to load all of the settings that we saved and set them in our game; this function will be used the most. Add this function to the bottom of the script:

```
public void LoadAll()
{
  SetSettings(PlayerPrefs.GetString("Custom_Settings"));
  ToggleShadows(PlayerPrefs.GetInt("Custom_Shadows"));
  SetFOV(PlayerPrefs.GetFloat("Custom_FOV"));
  SetResolution(PlayerPrefs.GetInt("Custom_Resolution"), PlayerPrefs.
GetInt("Custom_Full"));
  SetAA(PlayerPrefs.GetInt("Custom_AA"));
  SetVsync(PlayerPrefs.GetInt("Custom_Sync"));
}
```

In this function, we call each of the functions that we created and set them to the saved values. Since we use `PlayerPrefs` to save our configurations, we get the values from them.

Making audio configurations

For audio configurations, we'll set the volumes for background music, sound effects, and the atmospheric sounds. We will also be setting the speaker mode for the audio output. Let's start off by creating a new C# script and naming it `Audio_Config`.

Setting the values

The first function that we'll be creating will be used to set the default values for our configurations. Add this function to the script:

```
public void SetDefaults()
{
  SetBG(1.00f);
  SetSFX(0.80f);
  SetAtm(0.60f);
  SetAudioType("Stereo");
}
```

In this function, we call the functions that we'll be creating next to set the default values. For the first three functions, we set the volumes for various values. The last function sets the speaker mode to a stereo default.

Configuring the volumes

Now, we'll be adding the functionality to change the volumes. Add these functions to your script:

```
public void SetBG(float bgVolume)
{
  AudioSource[] audios = GameObject.FindObjectsOfType<AudioSource>();

  foreach(AudioSource source in audios)
  {
    source.volume = bgVolume;
  }
}
```

```
public void SetSFX(float sfxVolume)
{
  AudioSource[] audios = GameObject.FindObjectsOfType<AudioSource>();

  foreach(AudioSource source in audios)
  {
    source.volume = sfxVolume;
  }
}

public void SetAtm(float atmVolume)
{
  AudioSource[] audios = GameObject.FindObjectsOfType<AudioSource>();

  foreach(AudioSource source in audios)
  {
    source.volume = atmVolume;
  }
}
```

In each of the preceding functions, we pass a `float` variable, which will be the new volume. Next, we create an array of audio sources, which we will grab from the scene. Finally, for each of the audio sources, we assign its volume to the new volume value of our passed variable.

Setting the speaker mode

Next, we'll set the speaker mode for the audio output. This will affect how the player will hear your audio. A player who uses headphones might want to use surround sound. A player who uses speakers to hear your game may want to use the stereo sound instead. Add this function to the script:

```
public void SetAudioType(string SpeakerMode)
{
  switch(SpeakerMode)
  {
  case "Mono":
    AudioSettings.speakerMode = AudioSpeakerMode.Mono;
    break;
  case "Stereo":
    AudioSettings.speakerMode = AudioSpeakerMode.Stereo;
    break;
  case "Surround":
    AudioSettings.speakerMode = AudioSpeakerMode.Surround;
```

```
      break;
    case "Surround 5.1":
      AudioSettings.speakerMode = AudioSpeakerMode.Mode5point1;
      break;
    case "Surround 7.1":
      AudioSettings.speakerMode = AudioSpeakerMode.Mode7point1;
      break;
    }
  }
```

For this function, we pass a string, which will be used in a `switch` statement to change the speaker mode. In this `switch` statement, we check for each of the speaker modes that we want to support for our game. To change the speaker mode, we assign the `speakerMode` variable from `AudioSettings` and assign it to the associating speaker mode.

Creating the settings menu

The final part of our optimizations will be to add a menu so that the player can access and change the settings we created. Create a new C# script and name it `Config_GUI`.

Preparing the code

Now, we'll set up our code by adding variables, a `start` function, and an `OnGUI` function. Add this code to your script:

```
float volBG, volSFX, volATM, fov;
bool aa, shadows, sync, optionsGUI, full;
int res;
string settings, audiotype;
public Rect optionsRect = new Rect(100, 100, 500, 500);

void Start()
{
  volBG = 0;
  volATM = 0.3f;
  volSFX = 0.8f;
  fov = 90.00f;
  aa = true;
  fullscreen = true;
  shadows = true;
  optionsGUI = true;
  LoadAll();
```

```
  }

  void OnGUI()
  {
    if(optionsGUI)
    {
      optionsRect = GUI.Window(0, optionsRect, OptionsGUI, "Options");
    }
  }
```

All of the variables that we created are placeholders so that we aren't directly modifying the saved values that are in `PlayerPrefs`. The last variable, `Rect`, will be used to place and size our `Options` menu. In the `Start` function, we set the placeholders to some default values and call a `LoadAll` function. The `LoadAll` function will be created later; its purpose is to load our saved data in the placeholders. Finally, the `OnGUI` function will run the GUI window that will hold our `Options` menu.

Creating the GUI

Now, we will create the function that runs the GUI. We will create labels, buttons, horizontal sliders, and toggle buttons. Add this function to your script:

```
  void OptionsGUI(int gui)
  {
    GUILayout.BeginArea(new Rect(0, 50, 800, 800));

    GUI.Label(new Rect(25, 0, 100, 30), "Quality Settings");

    if(GUI.Button(new Rect(25, 20, 75, 20), "High"))
      GetComponent<Video_Config>().SetResolution(0, 3);
    if(GUI.Button(new Rect(100, 20, 75, 20), "Medium"))
      GetComponent<Video_Config>().SetResolution(1, 3);
    if(GUI.Button(new Rect(175, 20, 75, 20), "Low"))
      GetComponent<Video_Config>().SetResolution(2, 3);
    if(GUI.Button(new Rect(250, 20, 75, 20), "Custom"))
      GetComponent<Video_Config>().SetResolution(3, 3);

    GUI.Label(new Rect(25, 40, 100, 30), "Field of View");
    fov = GUI.HorizontalSlider(new Rect(115, 45, 100, 30), fov, 60.00f,
  120.00f);

    GUI.Label(new Rect(25, 60, 100, 30), "Antialiasing");
    aa = GUI.Toggle(new Rect(115, 60, 100, 30), aa, " On/Off");
```

```
GUI.Label(new Rect(25, 75, 100, 30), "Resolution");

if(GUI.Button(new Rect(25, 95, 75, 20), "1920x1080"))
   GetComponent<Video_Config>().SetResolution(0, 3);
if(GUI.Button(new Rect(100, 95, 75, 20), "1600x900"))
   GetComponent<Video_Config>().SetResolution(1, 3);
if(GUI.Button(new Rect(175, 95, 75, 20), "1280x1024"))
   GetComponent<Video_Config>().SetResolution(2, 3);
if(GUI.Button(new Rect(250, 95, 75, 20), "1280x800"))
   GetComponent<Video_Config>().SetResolution(3, 3);
if(GUI.Button(new Rect(325, 95, 75, 20), "640x400"))
   GetComponent<Video_Config>().SetResolution(4, 3);

GUI.Label(new Rect(25, 125, 100, 30), "FullScreen");
full = GUI.Toggle(new Rect(95, 125, 100, 30), fullscreen, " On/
Off");
```

For each option that we have, we make a block of code creating its label and buttons for the player to see and adjust. The label is being used as a title for the option, so the player knows what they are editing. The buttons are made available to change the setting when they are clicked. Changing the fullscreen option is done with a toggle button, which is a single button that can be turned on and off like a Boolean.

To adjust the field of view, we use a slider so that the player can scroll through many options. Using the slider adds more customization as you don't need to create buttons. A slider isn't ideal for all options, but it fits perfectly to adjust the field of view. Now let's continue to create the other options:

```
GUI.Label(new Rect(25, 140, 100, 30), "Shadows");
shadows = GUI.Toggle(new Rect(95, 140, 100, 30), shadows, " On/
Off");

GUI.Label(new Rect(25, 160, 150, 30), "Music Volume");
volBG = GUI.HorizontalSlider(new Rect(25, 180, 100, 30), volBG,
0.00f, 1.00f);
GUI.Label(new Rect(25, 200, 150, 30), "SFX Volume");
volSFX = GUI.HorizontalSlider(new Rect(25, 220, 100, 30), volSFX,
0.00f, 1.00f);
GUI.Label(new Rect(25, 240, 150, 30), "Atmospheric Volume");
volATM = GUI.HorizontalSlider(new Rect(25, 260, 100, 30), volATM,
0.00f, 1.00f);

GUI.Label(new Rect(25, 270, 100, 30), "Speaker Type");

if(GUI.Button(new Rect(25, 290, 75, 20), "Mono"))
```

```
    GetComponent<Audio_Config>().SetAudioType("Mono");
  if(GUI.Button(new Rect(100, 290, 75, 20), "Stereo"))
    GetComponent<Audio_Config>().SetAudioType("Stereo");
  if(GUI.Button(new Rect(175, 290, 75, 20), "Surround"))
    GetComponent<Audio_Config>().SetAudioType("Surround");
  if(GUI.Button(new Rect(250, 290, 100, 20), "Surround 5.1"))
    GetComponent<Audio_Config>().SetAudioType("Surround 5.1");
  if(GUI.Button(new Rect(350, 290, 100, 20), "Surround 7.1"))
    GetComponent<Audio_Config>().SetAudioType("Surround 7.1");

  if(GUI.Button(new Rect(25, 350, 100, 20), "Save Settings"))
    SaveAll();
  GUI.Button(new Rect(150, 350, 100, 20), "Back");

  GUILayout.EndArea();
}
```

There is a lot going on in this function, but it's all GUI code. To change the Quality Settings, Resolution, and Speaker Type parameters, we use buttons. When clicked, the buttons will call their associating functions for either the video or audio configuration scripts that we previously created.

To change the Field of View, Background Music volume, Sound Effects volume, and Atmospheric volume parameters, we use a horizontal slider to edit their values. For the Anti-aliasing, Fullscreen, and Shadows options, we use a toggle or radio button to switch them on or off.

Finally, we create a button that will save the settings, and another button to go back. The back button can be left open for now since it can be used to go back to the main menu or a pause menu.

Saving all the values

To save our settings, we need to create a function for it; let's do that now. Add this function to your script:

```
void SaveAll()
{
  PlayerPrefs.SetString("Custom_Settings", settings);

  if(shadows)
    PlayerPrefs.SetInt("Custom_Shadows", 1);
  else
    PlayerPrefs.SetInt("Custom_Shadows", 0);
```

```
PlayerPrefs.SetFloat("Custom_FOV", fov);

PlayerPrefs.SetInt("Custom_Resolution", res);

PlayerPrefs.SetInt("Custom_Full", Convert.ToInt32(fullscreen));

if(aa)
  PlayerPrefs.SetInt("Custom_AA", 1);
else
  PlayerPrefs.SetInt("Custom_AA", 0);

if(sync)
  PlayerPrefs.SetInt("Custom_Sync", 1);
else
  PlayerPrefs.SetInt("Custom_Sync", 0);

PlayerPrefs.SetFloat("atmVolume", volBG);
PlayerPrefs.SetFloat("sfxVolume", volSFX);
PlayerPrefs.SetFloat("bgVolume", volATM);
PlayerPrefs.SetString("audioType", audiotype);
}
```

What this function will do is use the `PlayerPrefs` function to save all of our values. To save the settings, we use the placeholder variables that we created earlier.

Loading all the values

The last feature of the `Config_GUI` script will be to load all of our saved data. Add this last function to your script:

```
void LoadAll()
{
  volBG = PlayerPrefs.GetFloat("bgVolume");
  volSFX = PlayerPrefs.GetFloat("sfxVolume");
  volATM = PlayerPrefs.GetFloat("atmVolume");
  fov = PlayerPrefs.GetFloat("Custom_FOV");
  aa = Convert.ToBoolean(PlayerPrefs.GetInt("Custom_AA"));
  shadows = Convert.ToBoolean(PlayerPrefs.GetInt("Custom_Shadows"));
  sync = Convert.ToBoolean(PlayerPrefs.GetInt("Custom_Sync"));
  fullscreen = Convert.ToBoolean(PlayerPrefs.GetInt("Custom_Full"));
  res = PlayerPrefs.GetInt("Custom_Resolution");
  settings = PlayerPrefs.GetString("Custom_Settings");
  audiotype = PlayerPrefs.GetString("audioType");
}
```

For each of the placeholder variables that we created, we load the saved data for it. To get the saved data, we use the PlayerPrefs get functionality to load the values.

Playtesting

For playtesting, try to change all of the values, saving and loading them. To make sure that the scripts work, just place all three scripts onto the same GameObject in every scene you have. For the quality settings, you will need to modify the native **Quality** settings in Unity. To do this, click on **Edit**, hover over **Project Settings**, and click on **Quality**. An **Inspector** window should appear on the right-hand side. Here, you will want to delete the default settings until there are three left, which will be **Low**, **Medium**, and **High**. It should look like this now:

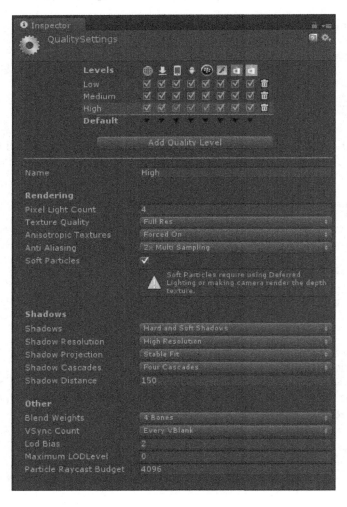

Summary

In this chapter, you learned how to create and save custom settings for your game. We created various settings for video as well as audio configurations. We then finally created a GUI menu to allow the player to modify the settings and optimize their game.

In the next chapter, we'll create a small game that will feature all of the gameplay features that we created throughout this book. By doing this, you will get a great example of how to implement everything you learned so far.

10
Putting It All Together

In this chapter, based on what you learned in the previous chapters, we will create a small game. We won't be using everything, but will use most of what you learned. This chapter will be a great exercise to help you learn how everything we created works.

In this chapter, you will learn how to:

- Create a main menu
- Create a few playable levels
- Implement character interactions
- Use sound effects and music
- Use the save and load features you created
- Implement enemy AI

Creating levels

In the game, there will be three playable levels and a main menu. The main menu will have three buttons on it: one to play the game, one for options, and a final one to exit the game.

The main menu

Create a new scene and name it Main Menu. Next, drag the Audio_Config, Video_Config, and Config_GUI scripts to the main camera. These will be used for our **Options** menu. Next, create a new C# script, name it MainMenu, and add this code to it:

```
void OnGUI()
{
  if(GetComponent<Config_GUI>().optionsGUI == false)
  {
    if(GUI.Button(new Rect(700, 400, 150, 50), "Play Game"))
      Application.LoadLevel("Chapter 10_a");
    if(GUI.Button(new Rect(700, 475, 150, 50), "Options"))
      GetComponent<Config_GUI>().optionsGUI = true;
    if(GUI.Button(new Rect(700, 550, 150, 50), "Quit Game"))
      Application.Quit();
  }

  GetComponent<Config_GUI>().OnGUI();
}
```

For this script, all that you will need is the OnGUI function. This code will create a few buttons that will be used to either play the game, show the options menu, or exit the game. Save this script and drag it to the main camera as well. When you run the scene, you should be able to see buttons similar to the ones shown in the following screenshot:

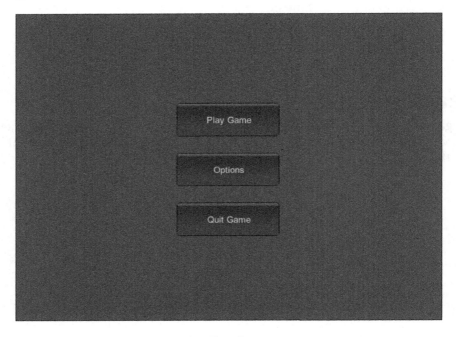

The playable level

We will create the level that we will play in. We will start off with creating just one level; once we start playtesting, we will clone the scene to make them. To make this simple, I'm using the scene from *Chapter 5, Enemy and Friendly AIs* and naming it Chapter 10_a. Doing this will give us a playable environment, as well as an enemy. Now, delete the main camera that is in the scene and drop in **First Person Controller**.

If you run the scene, you will see that the skeleton is tiny! This is because of its scale when it is imported to the engine. In the SkeletonData folder, click on the skeleton model. You will see the **Inspector** window open with the imported model data. In the **Scale Factor** property, change its value to 0.0225; this should make the skeleton look bigger. This value is the one that I am using, but feel free to use any value that looks good to you and fits the scene.

Now we need to make a few GameObjects and prefabs. First, we will create a gun for our player. Drop a cube primitive and scale it into a skinny rectangle. Move it up to the camera and place it where a gun typically is in an FPS. In the **Hierarchy** window, drag the **Gun** object and drop it on the main camera; this will force the gun to rotate with the camera. This is what the gun looks like on my **First Person Controller** object:

Next, drop a sphere; you can leave it as is, but I have put a material on it with a red diffuse color. Now drop the itemSelf script on it. These are the values that I have given to it:

- First Person Controller on the player slot
- **Amount** is set to 25
- **Value** is set to 30

- **Armor Amount** is set to 0
- **Weight** is set to 1
- **Name** is set to Potion
- **Stat** is set to Health
- **Self Action** is set to ChangeHP
- **Self Type** is set to Potion

Create a new prefab and name it Potion; now drop the sphere that you created on the prefab. You now have a prefab for health potions! Place two of these onto the map. Currently, you can't do anything with these potions, but later we will let the player pick them up.

Creating player interactions

Here, we will create ways for the player to interact with the game world. For our game, we will have the player shooting their gun, collecting potions, and pausing the game as interactions. Create a new C# script and name it PlayerInteraction. First, we will create a couple of variables and add them to our script:

```
public GameObject Projectile, Potion;
```

The Projectile GameObject will be the bullets that we shoot and the Potion GameObject will be the potion prefab that we created earlier.

Shooting and pausing

We will create the functionality to shoot the gun and pause the game. Add this Update function to your script:

```
void Update ()
{
if(Time.tmeScale != 0.00f)
{
  if(Input.GetButtonUp("Fire1"))
    Instantiate(Projectile, transform.position, transform.rotation);

  if(Input.GetButtonUp("Esc_Key"))
  {
    if(Time.timeScale != 0.00f)
      Time.timeScale = 0.00f;
```

```
    else
        Time.timeScale = 1.00f;
    }
  }
}
```

The first `if` statement will allow the player to shoot the projectile. To shoot it, we instantiate the GameObject and the player's location and rotation. To let the player pause the game, use an input that we created in *Chapter 1, Interactive Input*. Setting the `timeScale` object to `0` will pause any script that uses the `Update` function, and setting it to `1` will resume it.

Collecting potions

To collect potions, we will need to add a collision function, as follows:

```
void OnTriggerEnter(Collider other)
{
  if(other.tag == "Potion")
  {
    GetComponent<Inventory>().AddToInventory(1, Potion);

    for(int i = 0; i < GetComponent<GUI_2D>().Items.Count; i ++)
    {
      if(GetComponent<GUI_2D>().Items[i].name == "")
        GetComponent<GUI_2D>().Items[i] = Potion;
      break;
    }
    Destroy(other.gameObject);
  }
}
```

To collect the potion, we check the trigger's tag to make sure it is the potion. Next, we add it to the inventory by calling the `AddToInventory` function of the `Inventory` component, which we will be adding later. Also, we add it to the GUI by calling the `Items` array from the `GUI_2D` component and assigning the potion. Finally, we destroy the `GameObject` potion in the game world so that the player can no longer get that potion.

Adding all the sounds

Now we will add the background music and atmospheric sounds.

Playing the background music

Create a new empty GameObject and name it `Audio_Manager`. Drag-and-drop the `BG_Music_Manager` script on it. For this game, I will only use one song, so set the size of the **Song List** to 1 and add a song. If the volume isn't already set, set it to 1 as well. Before you can move on, you need to add an **Audio Source** component to this object. To do this, click on the **Add Component** button, click on the **Audio** option, and finally click on the **Audio Source** option.

Adding the atmospheric sounds

Next, we will add the atmospheric sounds. To do this, we will use a similar process as the background music. Create an empty GameObject and drag-and-drop the `ATM_Manager` script on it. Set the size of **TmpList** to 2 and add two sound clips. I am using *Open Space Wind1 – 32 Seconds* and *Open Space Wind2 – 36 Seconds* from the sound clips we got in *Chapter 8, Aural Integration*. Set the **Keys size** to 2, then set **Element 0** to `Wind1`, and **Element 1** to `Wind2`. If the volume isn't set, set it to `0.5`. Finally, add an **Audio Source** component to this GameObject as well.

Implementing the GUI

Now, we will add the 2D GUI that we created in *Chapter 2, GUI Time*.

Adding the script

Drag-and-drop the `GUI_2D` script onto the First Person Controller. Since we already have everything coded, your work is almost done for the GUI! In the scene, create a new empty GameObject and name it `Empty`; this will be used by the script. If you don't have default values for your `GUI_2D` script, set them to these values:

- **Current HP** to `100`
- **Max HP** to `100`
- **Current Bar Length** to `0`
- **Current Level** to `1`
- **Max Experience** to `100`
- **Current Experience** to `0`

- **Current Exp Bar Length** to 0
- **Max Exp Bar Length** to 100

With all of this added, when you run the scene it should look like this:

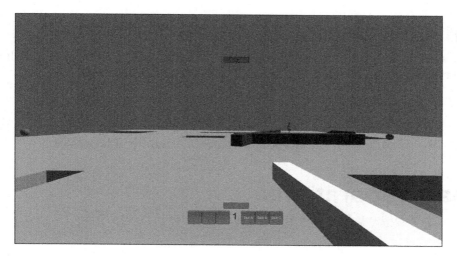

Tracking stats

Now we will add the stat tracking feature that we created in *Chapter 6, Keeping Score.*

Adding the script

To allow stat tracking, we will simply drag the StatTracker script and drop it on the main camera. Now, to show the menu for stats, we will need to add an Update function. Add this to your script:

```
void Update()
{
  if(Input.GetKeyUp(KeyCode.E))
  {
    if(showStats)
      showStats = false;
    else
      showStats = true;
  }
}
```

Now when the player presses the *E* key, it will toggle the showStats Boolean variable. The stats menu will only show when showStats is set to true.

Saving and loading

To let the player save and load data within our game, we will implement the save system that we created in *Chapter 7, Creating Save and Load Systems.*

Adding the script

Drag the `FLAT_Save_System` script and drop it on the main camera. There will be no default values for this script, so we will need to set them as follows:

- **SfileName** to `Test.txt`
- **Sdirectory** to `C:\Users\USERNAME\Desktop\`
- Drag-and-drop the **First Person Controller** onto the **Player** slot

Final preparations

Now, we will add our final features to make this game complete.

Adding win conditions

Right now, the game is playable, but there is no way to win! Let's change that by creating a new empty GameObject and naming it `RoundManager`. Next, create a new C# script, name it `WinConditions`, and add this code to the script:

```
public int Enemies;

void Start ()
{
  GameObject[] e = GameObject.FindGameObjectsWithTag("Enemy");
  Enemies = e.Length;
}

void Update ()
{
  if(Enemies <= 0)
  {
    if(Application.loadedLevel != 3)
      Application.LoadLevel(Application.loadedLevel + 1);
    else
      Application.LoadLevel(0);
  }
}
```

What this script will do is get a count of how many enemies there are in the scene and use that information to decide whether the player wins. In the `Start` function, we grab the amount of enemies and assign it to the `int` variable we created. In the `Update` function, we check that there are no more enemies left. In our game, when you kill all the enemies you move on to the next level; if there are no levels left, you return to the main menu.

Affecting the AI

In the `AI_Agent` script, we need to add these two lines of code to allow stat tracking and, as we just created, a way to affect the win conditions. Add these two lines to the `ChangeHealth` function just before you call the `Destroy` function:

```
Camera.main.GetComponent<StatTracker>().SetStat("Kills", 1);
GameObject.Find("RoundManager").GetComponent<WinConditions>().
Enemies--;
```

The first line will add to the `Kills` stat by 1, improving that stat. In the second line, we decrease the number of enemies, bringing the player one step closer to victory.

Finalizing the items

Just as with the AI code, we will need to modify another script to get the potions to work correctly. In the `GUI_2D` script, in the `OnGUI` function, replace the code for first `ItemButton` with this code:

```
if(GUI.Button(ItemButtons[0], Items[0].name))
{
   if(Items[0].name == "Potion")
   {
     Items[0].GetComponent<itemSelf>().selfType = SelfType.Potion;
     Items[0].GetComponent<itemSelf>().selfAction = SelfAction.
ChangeHP;
     Items[0].GetComponent<itemSelf>().Amount = 25;
   }
}
```

This code now makes that GUI button usable and will call the correct functions to use that potion.

Creating more levels

Now we come to the last step in making our game—making more levels! Since we have everything we need in our game added to this scene, we can just duplicate this scene and rename the new ones. I've duplicated the scene twice, naming one of them Chapter10_b and the other Chapter 10_c.

Playtesting

Before you can playtest the game, you have one last step to do. Click on **File** and go to **Build Settings**. You need to add all four of the scenes to the scenes in the **Build** section. To do this, select all of the scenes we are using and drag them into the empty section. It will look like this now:

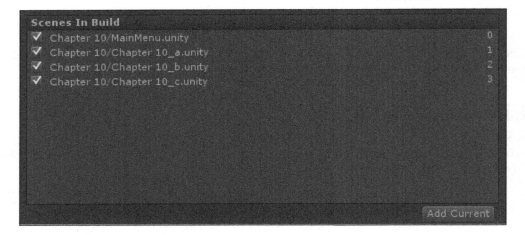

Now you can build out an executable and play the game! When building on a PC, you'll get an exe file along with a data folder; on a Mac, you'll get an app bundle. The game will start from the main menu, then you will have to play the rest of the levels to return to the main menu and beat the game.

Summary

Well, this is the end. This was the final chapter and it utilized all that we created in the previous chapters. In this book, you learned how to make a GUI system, create AI, create items, save and load game data, create a sound system, and much more. Then, using what you learned, you were able to create a short game demonstrating most of what we did throughout the book. Now is the time to move beyond this book and create your own games.

Index

U

Unity's NavMesh system 80
using statement 55, 140

V

values, audio configurations
  setting 155
values, settings menu
  loading 161
  saving 160
values, video configurations
  setting 150
variables
  adding 55, 56, 85
  initializing 143, 144
variables, atmospheric sounds
  creating 143
variables, melee item class
  adding 42
variables, projectile item class
  adding 45, 46
variables, self item class
  adding 40
variables, sound effects
  creating 145, 146
Vector3 variable 33
video configurations
  anti-aliasing property, toggling 153
  creating 150
  field of view, setting 151, 152
  quality settings, changing 154
  resolution, setting 152, 153
  settings, loading 154, 155
  shadows, toggling 150, 151
  values, setting 150
  vsync, setting 153
volumes
  configuring 155, 156
vsync
  setting 153

W

waypoint system
  used, for creating paths 80
win conditions
  adding 172, 173

X

Xbox 360 Controller
  about 5
  inputs, checking 7
XML
  enemy data, loading 132-134
  enemy data, saving 127-129
  loading with 130
  player data, loading 130, 131
  player data, saving 126, 127
  required variables, adding 125, 126
  saving with 125
XML files
  creating 123-125
XML save system
  about 123
  XML files, creating 123-125

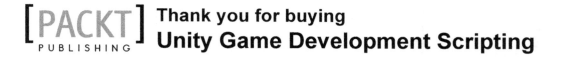

Thank you for buying
Unity Game Development Scripting

About Packt Publishing

Packt, pronounced 'packed', published its first book, *Mastering phpMyAdmin for Effective MySQL Management*, in April 2004, and subsequently continued to specialize in publishing highly focused books on specific technologies and solutions.

Our books and publications share the experiences of your fellow IT professionals in adapting and customizing today's systems, applications, and frameworks. Our solution-based books give you the knowledge and power to customize the software and technologies you're using to get the job done. Packt books are more specific and less general than the IT books you have seen in the past. Our unique business model allows us to bring you more focused information, giving you more of what you need to know, and less of what you don't.

Packt is a modern yet unique publishing company that focuses on producing quality, cutting-edge books for communities of developers, administrators, and newbies alike. For more information, please visit our website at www.packtpub.com.

Writing for Packt

We welcome all inquiries from people who are interested in authoring. Book proposals should be sent to author@packtpub.com. If your book idea is still at an early stage and you would like to discuss it first before writing a formal book proposal, then please contact us; one of our commissioning editors will get in touch with you.

We're not just looking for published authors; if you have strong technical skills but no writing experience, our experienced editors can help you develop a writing career, or simply get some additional reward for your expertise.

Learning C# by Developing Games with Unity 3D Beginner's Guide

ISBN: 978-1-84969-658-6   Paperback: 292 pages

Learn the fundamentals of C# to create scripts for your GameObjects

1. You've actually been creating scripts in your mind your whole life, you just didn't realize it. Apply this logical ability to write Unity C# scripts.

2. Learn how to use the two primary building blocks for writing scripts: the variable and the method. They're not mysterious or intimidating, just a simple form of substitution.

Getting Started with Unity

ISBN: 978-1-84969-584-8   Paperback: 170 pages

Learn how to use Unity by creating your very own "Outbreak" survival game while developing your essential skills

1. Use basic AI techniques to bring your game to life.

2. Learn how to use Mecanim; create states and manage them through scripting.

3. Use scripting to manage the graphical interface, collisions, animations, persistent data, or transitions between scenes.

Please check **www.PacktPub.com** for information on our titles

Unity 4.x Game AI Programming

ISBN: 978-1-84969-340-0   Paperback: 232 pages

Learn and implement game AI in Unity3D with a lot of sample projects and next-generation techniques to use in your Unity3D projects

1. A practical guide with step-by-step instructions and example projects to learn Unity3D scripting.

2. Learn pathfinding using A* algorithms as well as Unity3D pro features and navigation graphs.

3. Implement finite state machines (FSMs), path following, and steering algorithms.

Unity 4.x Cookbook

ISBN: 978-1-84969-042-3   Paperback: 386 pages

Over 100 recipes to spice up your Unity skills

1. A wide range of topics are covered, ranging in complexity, offering something for every Unity 4 game developer.

2. Every recipe provides step-by-step instructions, followed by an explanation of how it all works, and alternative approaches or refinements.

3. Book developed with the latest version of Unity (4.x).

Please check **www.PacktPub.com** for information on our titles

Made in the USA
Las Vegas, NV
19 December 2020